THE
QUINN ESSENTIALS
FOR WOMEN

a

9 Transformational Tools to

Accomplish Anything

By Andrea Quinn

Endorsements

"Andrea Quinn and her Quinn Essentials were the inspiration for me finding my voice and changing things for me. It was the first time I heard things put so simply and directly. When I truly implemented the tools and suggestions, everything changed. Andrea made me able to take on what I was always meant to do. I sent all my friends to Andrea's class, and I would love to take it again and again. I love her."

~ Brittany Snow, Actress, Producer, Director, Philanthropist

"Finally! The book thousands of us have been waiting for—from the manifesting coach of our dreams. My best friend and I took Andrea Quinn's legendary course a few years back, and she instantly met her dream man (now fiancé) while I had longtime goals realize within weeks. Whatever beautiful thing you're longing for, get ready to receive it and more."

~ Linda Sivertsen, Bestselling Author & Host of the Beautiful Writers Podcast

The Quinn Essentials for Women gave me the power to ask for what I wanted and the ability to receive it when it came. I'd long harbored a dream of becoming a professional writer and within a year of using Andrea's tools, I booked a job and became a member of the Writer's Guild of America. You must read this book.

~ Stephanie Allain, Award-winning Producer and Writer

"Tool #2 of The Quinn Essentials for Women rocked my world *and taught me a lesson I'll never forget.* "There is more power in your soul being visible than your personality." I cannot express how this theory (and Andrea's application of it) changed me. I've read a lot of books and taken a lot of courses, but this was a truly original concept that literally changed my life."

~Diane Luby Lane, Founder/Executive Director Get Lit - Words Ignite Producer, Literary Riot

"Andrea is so brilliant, so smart and has a big, beautiful heart for women who are ready to up level all areas of their lives. I had the great joy of being in one of Andrea's first live cohorts of The Quinn Essentials. Now the world will finally have access to these deep and transformative lessons that will set your life on fire, have you step into true Feminine Leadership and teach you how to create the legacy that you know is already in your soul. My suggestion: buy a few books for your best sister friends and go through The Quinn Essentials together and watch each other shine!"

~ Kim Coles, Actress, Comedian, Author, Speaker and Coach

"The Quinn Essentials are easy to implement tools that help you feel energized, inspired and unstoppable! I've used them when setting goals to level up my results. This book is a go-to guide, empowering and elevating women personally and professionally."

~ Angelica Rosas McDaniel, Raise Women Founder & TV Executive

"Andrea Quinn's Essentials…. is exactly that! An absolute essential for all women. Andrea assists you to dig deep to find the authentic you that has been there all along….and she does it with great style, humor, wisdom, and love. It's a must read!"

~ Linda Gray, Actress, Director, and Author "The Road to Happiness is Always Under Construction"

"Andrea Quinn is the real deal when it comes to empowering women. The Quinn Essentials are life-changing tools designed to make you happier, more confident, and more grounded. Run, do not walk, to read this book – and put what you learn into practice!"

~ Jaleh Bisharat, Co-Founder and CEO of NakedPoppy clean beauty

"The Quinn Essentials for Women helped me amplify the power I inherently knew I had but was too scared to express. The tools provided a road map that was easy to follow, and I recommend this for all women to experience!"

~ Natasha Des Ruisseaux, VP television network Executive

"The Quinn Essentials for Women - 9 transformational tools to accomplish anything lives up to its title! After implementing these life changing tools into my life - I feel energized and unstoppable. I recommend it to any woman who wants easy to understand nuggets that will transform you into a well-balanced, enlightened, and empowered woman."

~ Catherine Gray, Producer, Author, podcast Host, Founder SheANGELinvestors.com

"*The Quinn Essentials for Women* is perfect for anyone who craves a change in their life but has HAD IT with generic self-help books. Andrea Quinn came into my life like a supportive, loving bestie who intuitively guided me using a straightforward philosophical approach that, once hearing it, made it impossible to go back to pre AQ thinking. And because I like you, I'll give you a spoiler: everything you'll read in this book is stuff you already know. You just don't know it yet."

~ Ayser Salman, Author "The Wrong End of the Table"

"The Quinn Essentials for Women was life changing for me. The tools allowed me to walk into my power and use my voice. They are easy to implement and remember, which for me is a must! I also practice Andrea's tools within my family and my work family, and they have been incredibly impactful for all of us! *A must read!*"

~ Tami Pardee CEO/Founder Pardee Properties

"The life skill concepts, embedded in The Quinn Essentials, are a gift that keep on giving. I am consistently reminded of their relevance, truth, and power to thrive in everyday life. Andrea is a master teacher, sharing these principles with clarity, certainty, commitment, and contagious enthusiasm. I am forever grateful and excited that these tools are going to be shared with the world, because every woman deserves to receive them."

~ Marcy Cole, Ph.D. Holistic Psychotherapist, Wellness Educator, Life Enrichment Event Producer

"After utilizing The *Quinn Essentials,* I have knowledge about myself that's changed the Person I am today. I can't go back to being asleep at the wheel. I have Tools now. It really works."

~ Wendy Melvoin, Grammy, and Emmy winning Composer, Singer, Songwriter, Guitarist, Producer

"The Quinn Essentials for women have opened my eyes, shifted my life in a powerful way, and prepared me for a path of infinite possibilities. Andrea has a gift of guiding you, to navigate who you already are, with what you already have in front of you. Her enlightening words and lessons are pillars in my life, that I still practice to this day. Forever grateful for this journey."

~ Chonique Sneed, Musician, Choreographer, and Artistic Director

"The Quinn Essentials for Women transformed my life! Andrea's empowerment tools unlocked my courage - they allowed me to step into my power and achieve the life I envisioned. I recommend it to anyone who has a dream, a goal or wants to feel the power of their own strength and use it to make their dreams a reality."

~ Carolina Garcia, Director of Original Series at Netflix. Fortune 40 Under 40, HOLA! USA 2021 Latina Powerhouse Top 100

"Andrea's toolkit changed my life! Her empowerment tools re-framed a lot of things for me and helped me realize I had everything I needed at my fingertips. I recommend it to any woman who wants to understand how to make simple changes and tap into her own personal power."

~ Serena French, FASHION EDITOR, New York Post

"Andrea Quinn is a gift to me and so many of my clients! Every relationship in your life will be forever transformed with the guidance and wisdom of this book. The tools are easy to understand and will give you the confidence to accomplish your dreams and use your voice in the most powerfully feminine way. I like to refer to Andrea's book as 'a bible for women'. It will stay with you forever and you'll want to come back to it time and time again."

~ April Beyer, CEO & Founder LEVEL Connections, Matchmaker, Dating & Relationship Expert

The Quinn Essentials for Women

9 Transformational Tools to Accomplish Anything

By Andrea Quinn

ISBN-Electronic: 978-1-7347342-1-8

ISBN-Print: 978-1-7347342-0-1

Dedication

To my beautiful mother. You have been a beacon of
unconditional love every day of my life and who I aspire to be.
I am privileged to be a part of the circle of sacred women in our
family. You, grandma, your 8 sisters and 3 sisters-in-laws
are *mi grupo de mujeres amorosas* that are not only
my soul's foundation, but the catalyst for
my work with women.

Love you. Love you. Love you.

(*Happy me on the left with my family)

What Women Can be to Each Other

We can be sisters who lend an ear to listen
We can be a mother who has an open mind as well as a loving
heart
We can be a friend and give a shoulder to be cried on
We can give inspiration to one another
We can help each other realize a dream until it becomes a reality
We can be supportive of each other in joy and also in sorrow
We can teach each other while learning at the same time
We can be a helping hand to each other and expect nothing in
return
We can love each other for our greatness and in spite of our flaws
Most of all what we can be, to, for and because of each other,
are mentors, role models, and gifts from God
Be a Woman that you can look up to

Written by Evelyn Jackson – 2008
Published Poet in National Library of Poetry

Presented to The Quinn Essentials Women's Group 2008 as our
first Empowerment Speaker

Table of Contents

Preface

It was Fall of 2007 and I was completing my first year as a full-time life coach. So many things were happening. I was beginning a new chapter of my life, as my father was ending the last chapter of his. My father was a huge mentor to me, and I always found myself trying to get his approval as I grew up. He was a highly intelligent man with an intuition that was meant for wizards and warlocks (or so I thought). My father introduced me to so many great teachers and philosophies and was so committed to my education that he gave me homework every day after school. Even if I had homework from school, he thought it wasn't good enough and would add on his own exercises. It was such a volatile time in our economy back when I started coaching in September of 2006 that he was worried about me starting my own business. But for the first time in my life, my inner knowing trumped his.

I began to meditate and pray daily not only to cope with his upcoming transition, but to receive guidance to be the best advisor to the wonderful people who were showing up in my new coaching practice. Back in 2006, life coaching was not as popular as it is today, and I was grateful for the opportunity to be a support to so many who trusted me.

I have been a student of human development and behavior my whole life. I would read books that contained mental, physical, emotional and spiritual teachings from as many teachers and cultures as I could get my hands on. I was always searching because I was lost. There was so much about life that was confusing for me. I felt I was born with a special type of "knowing," but as far as using it to help myself, well that was a huge fail. I didn't trust myself, so I allowed my decisions to be made by listening to my family, especially my father. My own voice and knowing were drowned out by fear of life and fear of failure.

I had made some huge mistakes as a young woman. I always tell people, "If you've done it, I've done it bigger." To say I was malcontent is an understatement. Feeling trapped by my own life, I ran from everything I could. I was angry, bossy, controlling and rebellious.

One day in the mid-nineties, some friends asked me to go listen to a spiritual advisor who was visiting San Francisco from Japan. They said he was a master teacher and would have an interpreter. We were there to listen to him speak and then get in line to receive his assessment of you. When I got to the front of the line, he looked at me and said, "You have been given great power in this lifetime, not to fight others but to fight yourself."

Boom! My life was shifted from that day forward. I began studying deeper philosophy, psychology, theology, astrology, sociology, new thought, old thought, you name it...I knew that I had to develop an authentic relationship with myself if I was going to be happy. All that I was studying previously was so that I could better understand people, now it was time to study to better understand myself.

Back to 2007... As I was meditating and praying one morning, I felt the urge to create workshops to help women. I knew that I had followed a path and personal curriculum that was working for me. I finally was living a life I was loving, but as a work in progress, I was afraid to venture out to teach others, until my life was perfect (why do we do that?). As a woman, I was so hard on myself and had that bar set so high that I would never reach it. I needed to find the courage to move past my ego.

Every day when I would meditate, the same thing kept coming up, so after another grueling daily battle with myself, I finally surrendered my ego and grabbed a legal pad.

I began to write down my own version of a step-by-step curriculum that had changed my life. I took note of the work I did on my inner life and the work I did out in the world to get my life on track.

As I continued my daily work and meditation, the next thing I knew there were 9 transformational tools in a Toolkit. Where did this come from? I knew it had to have come from all my studying, but it was so clear and in order, it took me by surprise. For one of the first major times in my life, I followed my own knowing and decided it would be time to gather a few women to share my Toolkit. One night I had a dream and the name was given to me very clearly, "The Quinn Essentials." Wow! That's good! Who wrote that? I was so excited to continue now that I had a name and curriculum ready to go.

I reached out to 8 women who had seen me for coaching and asked them if they would like to join my class. To my surprise, they all said "Yes" without me even telling them what we were doing. (Personally, I don't think I would have ever done that!) So, on February 7, 2008, I held the first Quinn Essentials Accomplishment group workshop featuring the 9 tools in my living room. Before all the ladies arrived, I was on the phone with my father talking to him about the group of women that were coming over. Of course, he told me what to do, what to serve them and what to remember. I was grateful to have him on the phone with me that night being so lucid and powerful to guide me as he had done my entire life. It was one of the last powerful conversations we ever had. He was gone not too long after that night, but I felt he was with me every time I taught the tools.

The group was a success. These women from different walks of life came together and saw the magic within themselves and each other. It was one of the greatest things I had witnessed in my life. Those women gave me permission to continue with these tools and to step into my life's purpose.

It is why I wrote this book. This Toolkit contains my life's curriculum for women to accomplish anything. I have had the incredible privilege of having thousands of women apply these tools to change their lives. They have not only taken my workshop several times, but they have also brought their families, friends and co-workers to learn these 9 tools.

I had no idea how much these tools would change my life and the journey I would take with my Toolkit. I promise you will make a shift in reading this book and my wish for you is that you accomplish your dreams, receive happiness and create a life you love.

Andrea Quinn

September, 2021

Introduction
Opening the Toolkit

Here it is! Your Toolkit has arrived! This kit is filled with the 9 tools I know you can take with you the rest of your life to empower yourself and accomplish success in any area. I believe that women are great once they have the tools to succeed. I chose tools because they are action oriented, we have the choice to use them and with a little practice, we can build anything!

Women are the great creators. This world is populated because of women. Any person, male or female, who has ever lived on this planet started their lives in the womb of a woman. The true power that emanates from us is otherworldly. We are a divine collective of creativity, yet we are treating ourselves like scullery maids.

Women today have more power than we did in history, but it is coming at a very high price with little spiritual return. We women are painted into a corner, given the gold handcuffs, made to fight for our rights and personal choices, and are still expected to do everything for everyone. This is why I am sharing these tools with you. It doesn't have to be this way!

We women have an enormous amount of power and when we choose to harness it and use tools to transform our lives, it works. It has been my privilege to have thousands of women transform with these tools and I am excited you have chosen to read this book.

To receive the most from this book, I recommend using a notebook where you can keep track of your progress and explore the exercises in the Tools in Motion portion of each chapter. Each time I have taught a workshop with this curriculum I have required a notebook and I hear from women all the time that they refer to it year after year.

What are The Quinn Essentials?

The Quinn Essentials is an essential empowerment curriculum for women. A Toolkit filled with 9 transformational tools that are mental, physical, emotional and spiritual. When I talk about spiritual, I don't mean religious. Women from every religion have used these tools and they are applicable to their beliefs. In spiritual, what I am saying is how ever you define spiritual works for me. Some people define spiritual as Source, Universe, God, Goddess, Nature, Prime Creator, etc. Well, while I don't know your personal definition, I do know that if you were drawn to this book, you must believe somewhere inside of you there is an energy guiding you.

The tools are divided into three sections: *Everything on the Inside, Everything on the Outside* and *Bringing it all Together*. The first four tools are everything in your life I believe you must align with on the inside. It is your inner life. As I am sure you have heard before, "Life is an inside job." And if you don't have a strong inner life, then you won't be able to create or sustain a powerful outer life.

The next four tools are everything I believe you must align with out in the world to accomplish your dreams. They are more action oriented and are supported by the inner work you are doing in the first four tools. And the last tool brings them all together.

So, inner life essential tools, outer life essential tools and an essential integration that equals a balanced woman. When women are balanced, we are unstoppable! It's when we are blindsided by life and knocked off our axis that we become out of balance. This Toolkit rebalances you almost immediately.

Each one of us are struggling somewhere in life. We may have disempowering patterns and behaviors, low self-esteem, trauma and a myriad of other issues that keep us from living the life we want. I believe most of these issues are just habitual behaviors without the tools to navigate the situations that life delivers to us.

It is my commitment to empower women and give you tools to navigate any situation that comes your way. I take this curriculum very seriously. I share it with love and levity but that is to lighten what might be one of the hardest curriculums you have studied to date. With The Quinn Essentials, you will learn to have conversations with yourself to build a trusting relationship with YOU. There will be light bulb moments, laughter, 'good-to-know's and even a few tears. This Toolkit supports you through your growth and gives you a foundation to sustain what you are creating. Just like anything else if you work these tools – they work! These tools do not work themselves. You must be in partnership with The Quinn Essentials to create the life you want.

Accomplishments versus Goals.

To begin opening your Toolkit, you must know what you want to accomplish in your life. In my opinion, when you set an accomplishment for yourself, it is much broader than a goal. A goal is masculine and singularly focused, whereas an accomplishment is expansive and creative. Men can shut out the world, aim for their target and use their arrow (yes, that's what I mean) to achieve their goals.

On the other hand, women are multi-taskers who don't have the luxury of shutting everything out. On the way to our accomplishments, we still must take care of everything and everyone at the same time. When you look at your accomplishments, you will notice that you have already achieved so much; you have just been too busy to notice. We women believe if we don't have that one "goal" that we have been trying to achieve, then we have failed. The truth is the road to receiving our accomplishments is sprinkled with mini-accomplishments and we begin succeeding the minute we take the first step.

In this book, you will find a blank page titled, "Accomplishments." I would like you to start by writing three things you want to accomplish in your life. They can be anything. Here are some examples from other women who have used these tools.

I am accomplishing creating a home office.

I am accomplishing greater self-care.

I am accomplishing writing my novel.

I am accomplishing healing my anger from the divorce.

I am accomplishing receiving a promotion.

As you can see, it applies to any area of your life. I would like you to proclaim, *"I am accomplishing"* before each one. It is now a statement with power behind it. When you write your accomplishments, the tools in this book will aid you in manifesting them into a reality. One of the things that is great about accomplishments is that you don't have to know exactly how something will manifest. It begins to take on an energy all its own once you begin to give it awareness.

My Story

The Quinn Essentials all started because if there was anyone who needed tools to empower themselves, it was me. I was a woman who was #lost and a #mess. I have been married three times and had so many issues finding peace in my life and relationships. I was divorced and bankrupt before some of my friends had even gotten laid! With two failed marriages in my 20s, I seemed to attract situation after situation that put me in the "victim role." I had to make difficult choices, was judged harshly and felt powerless daily. I felt I had no friends I could trust, no money, had to move back in with my parents and lived as if I had a big "L" on my forehead. To top it all off, my ex-husband had taken my social security number and used it, without my knowing, to buy very expensive things, hence the bankruptcy. My life had taken on the tone of a soap opera, and I was spinning in a cyclone of drama and shame.

One of the things that saved me at the time was the studying of personal development that I was doing. As I mentioned, I was always a student of human behavior so the more I read, the more I would try to use what I was learning. But I quickly found out that knowing something intellectually and applying it are two different things. (Wow! If I just would have applied what I knew!)

I continued to make mistake after mistake. I had no idea what a relationship with myself looked like and all I cared about was getting approval from others. (But I had the knowledge.) I found myself married again to another man where again money was an issue. It was like I was on automatic pilot and was watching my life from the corner of the room. I had an eating disorder out of being a perfectionist and didn't take care of myself in the least. Like a lot of people, I could help anyone with their lives, but I couldn't help myself. That is why I took care of everyone else, to avoid me. Something had to give.

I began again to take classes from teachers on philosophy, spirituality and personal development. One day someone said in a workshop that "What you are asking of us is hard to apply in our everyday lives." That was it! It hit me like a frying pan. I wasn't applying what I knew. I was searching and searching for the answers, but I had them all along. I just wasn't applying them. It was that simple and that hard at the same time. That was literally what slammed on the brakes for me.

My life began to turn around because I was finally in the driver's seat. I was really good at paths, steps and tools. When I was given a roadmap, I could use it with success. That is why this curriculum and these tools are important for me to share because I promise that no matter what you are going through, have gone through or challenges you are currently facing, you will be able to take your power back.

I now live a life I love. I am married to an amazing man who has the patience, sense of humor and strength I require. I have a career I am grateful for every minute, authentic friendships, magical opportunities and an authentic and trusting relationship with myself. This didn't come easy and I still work on it every day. I use The Quinn Essentials from the moment I wake up until I go to sleep. My Toolkit saved me and continues to support me in every area of my life.

More Personal Sharing

This book is filled with a lot of personal stories. I use my own life as an example in many instances because it is the only life I can talk about with full authority. I share stories about my husband Chris, my mom "Lovie," my family and friends. Every chapter also has "Success Stories" from women who have used The Quinn Essentials over the years. How I perceive my experiences are meant to be an example so that you might relate to it in your own life.

I tell women when I teach my workshops that whatever mistakes you think you made, I made them bigger. I was the queen (or Quinn) of sabotage. I want to stress to you that if I can create the life I am living, you can create or recreate yours.

One More Thing

Your life and dreams are sacred to me. Giving you these tools through this book is a dream come true for me. In this book, I speak to both male-female relationships and female-female relationships. My intention is always inclusivity. I honor that each soul manifests a life of experience in many different ways and if I haven't shared an example you can relate to in your life, then try to go under the story to the essence of what I am sharing.

I also speak about men. I love men (which is why I married so many). I am not against men. I just understand our inherent differences. We are different. We should have the equal rights and opportunities but physically and mentally, we are different. You'll find I speak to those differences with an honoring to each gender.

Anyone who knows me, knows I am passionate regarding the honoring, empowerment and success of women. We are all souls trying to navigate this life and look through different lenses, but at the core, we are more alike than we are different. We, as women, are sacred creators and with these tools, I wish for you an empowered life of dreams realized, healed hearts and accomplishments received.

Now let's open up this Toolkit!

Accomplishments

List 3 things you want to accomplish here:

Section One

Everything on the Inside

Chapter I

RECEIVE

Why try to be a King
when you're already the Queen!

Welcome to the first Tool in The Quinn Essentials Toolkit – **Receive**.

To accomplish the life you truly want, you must first receive it. The dilemma that we so often have as women is that we are the "doers," which is actually counterproductive to who we are as Creators.

I want to invite you to now begin to recognize how everything a woman does is actually a part of the creative process. Whether you are receiving love in order to create a relationship, receiving funding to create a business, receiving connection to others to create community, physically receiving to create a child, or receiving whatever you require to create healing – it's all in Receiving.

That is because receiving is your BIRTHRIGHT as a female.

As women, we are born receivers, not only physically, due to our anatomy, but energetically as well. Simply put, we are born to do one thing and one thing only – **Receive to Create.**

Now, take a deep breath... Congratulations! By receiving air into your body, you have just received the in-breath of your life to create the exhalation. This is the first step in understanding this tool; receiving on the in-breath and creating on the out-breath. (*That's it... Breathe... Okay, now exhale. Now, keep breathing – because I know you probably stopped and are holding your breath as you're reading this book right now.*)

The issue that so many women face is that they have no idea how to receive, but they definitely know how to "Do." All the "doing" in the world does nothing but make you tired, resentful, bitter and angry. Have you noticed?

This first tool can be challenging, but when you get it down, it begins to change your life in some of the most powerful ways. I know some of you overachievers may be shaking your heads right now. But I promise you that, when you grasp this concept, you will understand that for all you have "done" to achieve in your life so far, when you start receiving, you will accomplish more than you could have ever wished for.

I hate to burst your bubble, you're not a doer.

When I say this in my workshops, I get a lot of what we call in my house, "German Shepherd Head." (*This is where our dogs cock their heads side to side as if to ask, "What are you talking about?"*) Women think that the more they do, the more they will accomplish or the more they will be loved. If that sounds familiar to you, let me ask you, "How's that been working for you?"

We women fear that by not doing and switching to receiving, it somehow makes us seen as weaker or passive in some way. But, in fact, when you are being who you have come here to be – a receiver to create – you are more powerful than you or anyone else can even imagine. As a receiver, you align yourself with the truth of who you really are.

Just ask yourself if you'd rather be King Richard the Lionhearted who took his sword and went to battle or Queen Elizabeth I who made ALL the rules, entertained many male courtiers, created peace, supported the arts and received to create a powerful kingdom? Receiving to create IS true Feminine Power. This isn't Princess Training.

The fact is that, as a female, your body was engineered to receive the seed to create life. You were quite literally built to receive. This has nothing to do with sexual preference or orientation. Simply put, you are physically and emotionally coded in your DNA to receive and the reason – the only reason – you are here is to receive to create. That also means that creativity is your superpower! Therefore, Anatomy 101, no matter how badly you may want it, if you look down in your pants, there is no sword.

I get how hard this can be. I really do. All too often society has taught us to put everyone else's needs before our own. And as a woman, it's been drilled into our psyche that it's better to give than receive. (*How many times have we all heard this one?*) This is the number one reason why women feel out of alignment with who they are and why they keep themselves from accomplishing what they truly desire.

I work with a lot of very powerful women who when they first come to see me are "doers." But, after finishing my course, these CEOs and presidents of major companies say to me, "Wow, if I would have done this earlier in my career, I would be chairman of the board already."

I'm not saying you can't get to where you want to go by doing. What I am saying is that you're not going to get to the level you could achieve with true power. And then the next question is can you sustain your success?

All the doing in the world does nothing but drain your energy and precious life force. Because here's the thing, ladies, receiving to create is anatomical. It's archetypical. It's truth. My hope is to end your habit of constant *doing* so you may *receive* more than you ever dreamed.

Are you squirming yet?

Receiving is the gateway to all you desire.

We've looked at the physical body, now we're going to look at relationships.

Archetypically, the woman is a Goddess (I know you may not identify yourself that way nor feel it at this moment – JUST STAY WITH ME) and the man is a Knight.

I know talking about women as goddesses has become a bit trendy and, to be honest, a little bit overused. However, I used it before it was trendy and am using it now with you because I deeply believe that being a Goddess is our innate essence. The Goddess receives to create life while the Knight carries the sword to protect and be of service. And out of that we have a population! (*We may not need men to raise children, but we do need men to help us create them... That's just a fact.*)

Here's an example of the inherent differences between a woman and a man in the workplace. Both women and men write screenplays. The process for the female is that she received the idea through inspiration to create the story. The male protects the idea and is in service with his story. They both accessed their creativity through their archetypical process. The female created through receiving; the male created through service but they both got to completion. See where we are going?

When you finally realize the difference between receiving to create versus protecting and serving, you will have the 'aha' moment that you are "doing too much." You are a receiver! Put down the sword!

Is everybody getting your energy but you in your own life? Are other friends finding love? Are co-workers getting promoted who are not "doing" as much as you? Then just take a deep breath (because I know you are still holding it as you are reading this book) and begin to open your mind to receiving.

This is the tricky part... Women have been trained for generations to be doers as if to pay some type of penance to receive. Somewhere, somehow, we were taught that we needed to be submissive to take our place in a patriarchal culture to get what we want. So, when women began to stand up for themselves to be heard and recognized as voters, as leaders and people of influence, the mantra became, "I can do it all. I can open my own doors – thank you very much. I am woman and not only do I roar, but I can bring home the bacon, cook it, clean up after it, raise children, build an empire, take care of everyone, have multiple orgasms and all on as little sleep as possible so tomorrow I can do it all again!"

THIS IS A FANTASY AND IT DOES NOT WORK! (In fact, when you start doing it all and giving it all, the "takers" show up. Haven't you noticed?)

What I know for sure is that when you start receiving, the givers begin to show up! The problem is that most women are uncomfortable with all this energy coming towards them and can begin to feel out of control instead of empowered. You will have to get used to this type of energetic shift. The true gift of receiving is being supported so you can create and not control. The practice of controlling our environment is something we women have habitually done out of not feeling safe in our lives. Along the course of history, women have felt the need to carry the sword (understandably) to get their just desserts. But to really have our cake, we need to put down that sword. It doesn't belong to you.

And the only thing it will do is hold you back from your true nature because receiving truly is the gateway to all you desire.

Women today are more exhausted than ever, and this speaks to how much "doing" is really going on. We are getting sicker at younger ages than the generations before us. This is inherently because of the amount of weight we are carrying as "those who do it all."

I am fortunate to coach many types of couples and I can tell you that in couples coaching it is about what you want to build/create together. Navigating relationship problems is what couples therapy is about, which I highly recommend when needed, it just isn't what I do.

In a relationship with a male (I'll go into a relationship with a female next), the problem is you're doing everything instead of receiving everything. Our culture has precisely constructed a dynamic where the woman does everything to prove her value and "earn her independence." It's going to take YOU to interrupt this pattern.

The good news is that your mate, the Knight, is there to protect and be of service to you, the Goddess. You are not there to take care of him and when you go into the practice of being the caretaker/mother, you are not in the receiving mode. Being taken care of is not why men initially enter relationships. Since we as females are coded to receive and they as males are coded to protect and serve, when you do enact a caretaker role, both of you will find yourselves operating from a less powerful position. But, when we allow our Knights to pick up the swords and fulfill their nature to protect and be of service, we return to our power position as the receiver and elevate the potential of our partnerships.

Now, let's take a moment to look at female/female relationships. Guess what, you are both receivers! And your job is to receive to create this relationship or anything else that you two are creating together. When two women come to see me, sit together and begin talking about creating for their families, careers, or lives in general, the entire energy becomes so powerful that solutions become effortless and the alignment divine.

Creativity is the female superpower.

The truth is there are only two places that we exist. We are either in resistance or we are in alignment. Women have been taught to push, push, keep pushing, get your goals, keep going, going, going. And so, we find ourselves exhausted, angry and resentful that everyone else's dreams are coming true and ours aren't. Or everybody else's projects are being funded but not ours.

Here's where I'm going to ask you to consider releasing resistance in your life.

Have you ever heard a woman say, "Oh, my God, all I did today was create, create, create and I'm exhausted!"? I'm going to bet you haven't. You know why? Because when a woman creates all day long, she's exhilarated. When a woman creates all day long, she starts at 10:00 AM, and she can't believe it's 8:00 PM already.

We've all had those glorious moments where we're just in the flow – cooking a meal, painting, writing a song, or planting a garden. That's the flow of creativity! That is the feminine superpower! When you're in the flow, you are in alignment with the truth of who you are. Time is irrelevant. And chances are you're energized beyond belief and not exhausted. But, when you're doing, doing, doing all day long, you can barely pick yourself up off the floor.

I know how difficult it can be to break a habit. Believe me when I say I know it's going to be much easier in theory than it is to put this into practice. That's because it's been a pattern to always "do" and now you're learning the new pattern of receiving. I promise you that if you stay with this, you're going to end up being able to do so much more for so many others as well as for yourself. And because you're going to be creating it from an authentic place, you won't be as tired anymore.

I personally still must practice receiving all the time. I will say to my husband, "I'm the receiver" and when he replies with, "I know that" I then say, "I know, I'm saying it for me." What I'm doing is reminding myself to interrupt my own pattern of controlling. As women, we think everyone does it wrong (especially men) so if we just do it ourselves, then it will be done right. However, I'm here to tell you that when we say, "Oh, I'll just do it anyway," we are just fooling ourselves. We are not only being control freaks, but this behavior is also costing us the precious energy we could channel to create what we truly want in our lives.

Because, without receiving as a doer, you are going to have to sacrifice somewhere; sacrifice your energy, sacrifice your time, sacrifice something. However, when you're in receiver mode, energy and momentum start coming to you and you'll be able to experience expansion firsthand.

Everything is in the receiving.

When you can really hold that space for yourself and begin to see yourself as a receiver, so will everyone else. You'll start to notice how things get a little easier day by day. It sounds impossible (*and a little crazy maybe*) but it works.

That's because the bigger the in-breath, the bigger the out-breath and the more you receive, the more you will be able to give authentically. Women love to give, but when you give from a place of exhaustion, it's not authentic. It's obligation. However, you can begin to flip these things around by remembering who you are, a receiver, a Creator. Doing so isn't selfish. It's authentically who you are.

Let's say you're the boss and you have a critical issue at work. Before you may have asked, "What do I have to do to fix this?" Instead, you'll now ask questions like: Who could I **receive** assistance from that could align me with getting this thing handled? Who could I **receive** assistance from to help me expand my business? Or what could I **receive** right now that would take me one step closer to my success? Asking the questions "what could I receive?' or "who could I receive from?" will put you back into alignment and out of the habit of "doing."

Success Story #1

I had a woman in one of my groups who was the then very rare-to-find president of a film company in Los Angeles. She was very powerful and had won Oscars. I would say to her, "You are kind of a big deal" and she would laugh about it because it was true.

While she was learning about receiving, she was also thinking about how much she had to fight and struggle to get to where she was in her career. She had always been the lone girl with all the boys at the top doing her thing, but it had also come at a very high price.

When she told us this story in her group the month after learning the Receive tool, she kicked it off with, "This receiving shit works!" She told us how for the first time in her career, she had put the sword down.

The day after she had learned about receiving, she had an important meeting with a group of investors for a big, big film. While the all-male investor group was waiting in the conference room, she had been in her office pacing because she had to deliver the news to the investors that the project they were meeting about was not going to work at all.

At that moment, there was no way they could make money from the production because there were some obstacles that she could not see hurdling. (I want to add that she is one of the most intelligent and respected people in filmmaking and most people come to her to solve their problems with productions, so if she couldn't figure it out, it was probably a lost cause.) But they had all come in, the meeting was about to start, and now she had to join them.

She said it was at that moment she heard my voice say, "Put the sword down and receive!"

So, she walked into the boardroom of all men – except for a female assistant in the corner (which is changing, and we must create more seats at the table for females) – and said, "Hello, gentlemen, before we get started, I would like to **receive** your assistance with something that I need to figure out."

She told us that she swore she heard a whole group of swords in the boardroom come up just like that. Wooosh!

She had never in her life felt so supported as she said to them, "Here's what's happening. I'm looking to **receive** a solution to this one particular issue on a film I am working on." Not letting them know it was the one they had invested in, she proceeded to give them a similar situation to the one she knew they were facing.

One guy piped up and said, "Well, you should do this and this..." and then another guy responded and said, "Well, what about that and that...?" And as people were starting to make suggestions, boom, she received the solution she needed!

When she was ready, she said to this boardroom of Knights, "Thank you all so much! Now we can get started with our project. Here's how it's going to go..." and she laid it all out for them with her own clever tweaks.

Not only did the film get fixed, not only did it get financed, but both sides made more money than they were initially supposed to.

She knew it was because she had put her sword down. She didn't assume that she had to figure it all out herself. Instead, she had asked to receive assistance with something so that she could create what she needed. When she was receiving, she was open to the solution without ego and received the solution by listening to others. In doing so, she did not feel weak in any way – in fact, she felt strong, supported and energized!

I have heard this same refrain over and over from powerful women who have implemented receiving practices into their business because what I'm sharing with you here works.

**Receiving never weakens you,
it only makes you more powerful.**

What I'm asking of you will never weaken you. It will only empower you. Receiving empowers you to be supported and to take care of your creative energy so that you can be more powerful, be more successful and have the things you want, whatever they are. Maybe it's to have a more successful love relationship. To have an expansive business. Or to be the best teacher you can be. Whatever it is for you, it will only come out of receiving and through receiving, you will be able to create more opportunities.

It cannot come out of forward movement alone. You must bring the energy in to you first (think in-breath) so that you can bring it forward with such creative force that your life ends up looking like you want it to effortlessly (think out-breath).

Effortless is, in fact, one of my favorite words. When you combine effortlessness with the empowerment of recognizing your feminine imprint as that of a receiver, you have the foundation necessary for true creation. It's all in the art of non-resistance.

Author and creativity expert Steven Pressfield said, "Most of us have two lives: the life we live and the unlived life within us. Between the two, stands resistance." Resistance is an ego-driven forcefield that keeps you stagnant and small. Effortlessness and empowerment cannot exist alongside resistance, nor can receiving because resistance repels receiving. But once you begin the steps of receiving – starting with the in-breath – you are not in resistance anymore and you will find yourself in alignment with the very simple foundation of your biological birthright.

It starts with when you wake up and the first thing you say to yourself is, "I intend to receive an effortless day." Or another one I love is, "I am open to receiving today." Maybe we don't even know what that looks like, but that's okay. Simply acknowledging being the receiver is enough. When you start aligning with receiving, things will start coming towards you.

Success Story #2

In another workshop, on the night we finished discussing receiving, I noticed one of the women getting quite agitated and so I asked her what was going on. She said, "Mama's going home..." I wasn't quite sure what that meant but I could see that something had clicked for her in a new way.

When she returned the following month for the next tool, she shared with us that she had realized she was living with four Knights (her husband and 3 sons) and that she was not the Receiver but the Uber-Doer in the family. So, when she got home that night, she called all of them to the table and said, "Things are changing in this family as of tonight!" She let them know that she was the receiver, and that this family was set up for everyone else to succeed but her.

She told them that she needed to receive so she could create a thriving home environment for them, but they had to be of service to make this happen. She then told each of them, including her husband, what she was to receive from them.

She couldn't believe how well it worked! When she told us all the story, it had been 30 days and counting and things had improved so much for her. She now had so much more energy and creativity that she actually signed up to join her church choir, something which she had not had the time to do in the past. She also told the group how the way she asked herself questions in terms of receiving played a large part in the transformation of her daily life.

What Story #2 illustrates is the importance of understanding your value and becoming aware of where you want to receive support so that you can create your greatest life and that the questions you ask yourself during the process matter.

Inhale, Receive – Exhale, Create.

Let me ask you this, which of the following questions sounds more powerful to you: "What can I do to fix this mess?" or "What can I receive that would support me in fixing this problem?"

Can you feel the difference? To me, the first one feels exhausting just reading it.

That's because when you ask the first one, you're focused on the doing and are going it alone. The second question is so much more powerful because it is focused on receiving and support. That shift is what begins to move your life in the way that you as a female are meant to live. Questions addressed from a place of receiving bring the energy to you and reveal the answers, relationships, opportunities and the life that you're meant to create.

For most women, receiving is the most challenging tool to integrate. Most of the time, we don't even breathe deeply. Instead, we take short breaths in all areas of our lives, which tends to put us in survival mode. (*Hello, multitasking!*) We become breathless from all we try to do and eventually run out of air so there's nothing left for the out-breath of creation. The doing has gotten in the way of our true creating. Then what happens? We feel "off" or exhausted or unhappy or stressed or at loose ends.

This will come as no surprise, but most women even have a hard time receiving a compliment, let alone receiving their best lives. Have you ever noticed how sometimes when you compliment a woman, she rarely stops to take it in or receive it?

For instance, when you compliment a woman on a blouse she's wearing, does she rush to tell you she got it at Target for $7.99? Think about it... What do you do when someone tosses a compliment your way? What happens when a woman tells you she likes your hair? Do you reply with, "Really? I didn't wash it today."

47

or "It's not as gorgeous as yours." Ask yourself, do you deflect, deflect, deflect?

I say, "Really, ladies?!?" The proper response is "Thank you."

Then stop and take an in-breath because you must be able to fully take in or receive the small things to get you prepared to receive those big things that you really want in your life.

You may be successful plugging away the way you always have. Many women are. But your true power comes from being in alignment with who you are, and that true power begins with a full breath in to receive, followed by exhaling full energy out to create.

After many years of seeing these tools work for thousands of women from all walks of life, I can tell you with certainty that if something is wrong in your life, you are not receiving somewhere. It is as simple as that. I don't know where it is that you are not receiving, but I know for sure that if there is a problem in your life, you are not receiving something in some way.

Let's start right now. First, take an in-breath and think "Receive."

Next, exhale and think "Create."

Ask yourself, in accomplishing your dreams, what is the first thing you could receive that will start you on your path? Where do you notice that you could receive more support?

This is just the beginning! Take it slow and let's start taking some small steps towards how to Receive right now!

Tools in Motion

1. Begin with simply acknowledging that you are a receiver. Take a deep breath and say to yourself, "I'm a receiver." Now sit still, close your eyes and say it again. With your eyes closed, see the energy moving to you as you take a deep breath and say it again.

Jot down your feelings about that statement. Ask yourself if it gives you energy or does it make your inner critic show up and start telling you all the ways this can't work for you? Keep repeating "I am a receiver" over and over as a reminder of your truth (even if you don't believe it yet). In the beginning of using this tool, your mind will be doubting, questioning and judging but your body will understand what you are asking.

2. Add "receive" into your vocabulary by using some easy-to-use phrases like:

"I would like to receive a moment of your time." "I would like to receive assistance with this project."

"I would appreciate receiving some help with cleaning the house." "I would like to receive a low-fat latte with an extra shot."

(You may feel silly using it at first but no one else will notice.)

3. Begin every morning for the next 30 days by joyfully asking the question:

"What one thing can I receive this morning that would make this day effortless for me?"

Record your feelings around this and watch a shift take place in your comfort levels. Feel free to add more receiving questions of your own, but even using this one particular question can be life changing.

4. Go back to your list of three accomplishments that you chose for yourself in "Opening the Toolkit." Next, ask what you can receive to realize those accomplishments, i.e. "What can I receive to_____?"

5. This exercise is one that is a great barometer on where you are as a receiver... When you go to the market to buy groceries and the person who is bagging your items at the checkout asks you if you would like to assistance to your car, reply with, "Yes, thank you."

Try to have fun with it, even if you're squirming a bit, and receive as you walk alongside him/her to your car. Keep in mind that if you can't receive free assistance with your grocery bags, how will you truly receive your life's accomplishments! (*You might not go grocery shopping or have a car to carry out to but get creative and notice where you resist being assisted. Awareness is very important with this tool.*)

6. Replace your "To Do" list with a "To Receive" list.

Good to Know

1. I hate to burst your bubble, you're not a doer.

2. Receiving is the gateway to all you desire.

3. Creativity is the female superpower.

4. Everything is in the receiving.

5. Receiving never weakens you, it only makes you more powerful.

6. Inhale, Receive – Exhale, Create.

Continuing the Conversation

For a deeper dive into this tool, please join me for a video which will assist you in implementing receiving into your life.

http://www.thequinnessentials.com/receive/

or scan QR code

Chapter II

I AM

Q

Choose Soul visibility over a shiny personality.

Tool Number Two, **I AM**, is one of my favorites in The Quinn Essentials Toolkit because it has changed so many people's lives. This second tool is more of a spiritual tool. For this tool, I am going to ask you to put your "humanness" aside. I will cover personality and your "humanness" in Tool #4, but for now this is all Soul!

As I mentioned in the intro to this book, the first four tools are what I believe you must align with on the "inside" to accomplish your dreams – and this tool takes us deep inside to the soul level. This tool is used to align yourself with your true power as a foundation that will support you and your dreams the rest of your life. It is your inner life that we are going to begin to explore with this tool and this is a game changer so you might want to read this chapter a couple of times.

I AM is the truth of who you are at the soul level. It has nothing to do with your personality, your mind, or your talents. It has everything to do with your soul and its greatness. It is also your pure awareness of being. While I am not personally religious, some of the tools in The Quinn Essentials Toolkit are more spiritual than others. I AM is one of them.

It is greater than your personality, your thoughts and your talents! Discovering and accessing your I AMs will give you true power. The core of what I'm talking about here is source energy. What is source energy? It is your life force and is often called many other things such as God, Goddess, Light and Universal Mind to name a few. Whatever you want to call that connection is entirely up to you but for this purpose, I will call it Source or Universe.

Your I AMs are the truth of who you are from birth. Every person is born with I AMs as their direct connection to Source. The most profound part of this tool is that it both makes your soul visible and your connection to that Source tangible.

Unfortunately, we often put our personality at the forefront and don't dig deep enough into what's beneath. However, when we do dig a little deeper and allow our soul to be made visible (versus letting our personalities run the show), we become much more successful in accomplishing our dreams.

No matter how we use the words I AM in a sentence, it begins to access creation. It becomes that powerful of a statement, which is why you must be very mindful when using I AM. Can you see that when we use it in negative terms, it can create what we don't want to receive as well. I AM fat, I AM poor. I AM so stupid. I AM broken. We must stop using those two words together as anything but powerful.

I AM is your connection to greatness.

I AM is your connection to something greater than being human. It is the truth of who we really are when we were born before shit got real and before life dealt us the hands we are now playing. When we understand how to navigate from that place, no longer stopped by our ego or our fears, we become unstoppable. So, let's get into the fun stuff... finding your personal I AMs.

I want you to think as far back as you can remember to who you were when things still felt magical. Think about what you were like when you were five, six, or even seven years old before life got in the way.

Remember her for a moment. Remember when she was singing into her hairbrush? Remember when she would paint like Picasso and put them all up around the house because they were fabulous? Remember when she played baseball with the boys and was the best on the team? Or when she cut off Barbie's hair and gave Barbie her first Mohawk? You thought she was amazing, right?

Guess what... That's who you really are! You are not the tired female who's been dealt a raw deal and is trying to struggle through it.

You are THAT fabulous girl from your childhood!
Before you can access the true power of this tool, you must create your I AM statements. It is imperative to have them in front of you

while reading the rest of this chapter so you can begin to see how to use them in your everyday life.

To bring your I AMs to light, we will be going underneath your personality traits and from there create your top five I AM statements. Do you have ten? Yes. Do you have fifteen? Of course, you do. But your predominant 5 are your own personal five-point star foundation.

Your I AMs only come from pure light so they cannot be any "bad traits." ("Bad traits" are human and do not come from your soul!) To help better understand how to discover your own I AM statements, I will give you my five I AM statements as an example and how I got to them.

These are mine:

I AM Kindness

I AM Intelligence

I AM Generosity

I AM Loyalty

I AM Sensitivity

When I go back to when I was a little girl, before I became immersed in my personality (outgoing, dramatic, bossy, sometimes bitchy, controlling, emotional, etc.), I can tell you the first thing that I remember about "little" me is that **I AM Kindness**.

I was always kind. I was the girl who didn't want you to put ladybugs in a jar because they couldn't go home for dinner and their mom was going to worry about them. I cried if you stepped on ants. I would hug strangers in the grocery store and freak my mom out. That was my soul being made visible.

It even showed up on my first Valentine's Day in kindergarten. I was the girl who brought Valentines for everybody, even the kid everyone called "Stinky Jimmy." (Remember kids who had nicknames like "Stinky Jimmy" and how children could be so mean?) I was horrified that some kids didn't bring valentines for other kids, and I became so upset that my parents had to console me all evening after school to calm me down. That's how bad I felt.

But I AM Kindness so, the next year I made my mother buy me extra valentines to put in my bag in case it happened again. If it did, I would give them one of my extra valentines and tell them to give it to Stinky Jimmy (this is where the #bossy and #controlling might have begun).

Now, I didn't say I was kind (that is a human trait). I said I was Kindness. This is because my soul resonates kindness. That kindness then translates into a kind human. (Not to worry, if you're still unsure. Stay with me and by the end of this chapter, you will get it!)

My second one is **I AM Intelligence**. I don't know how I know half of what I know, I just know it. I always have. I came into the world this way.

When I was a little girl, I was like the Hermione Granger of my class. Someone would say something, and I'd instantly pipe up with, "I know!" How did I know? I don't know, but I did, and I do. Intelligence shows up in different ways for people and my soul radiates an intelligence that translates into a woman who is intelligent in my way. All I AMs start at the soul level and then translates through us as women. (Also, it is very important that women acknowledge their intelligence.) So, I AM Intelligence.

I AM Generosity. I remember having playdates in my room and people would say, "Oh, I love this dress." That's all I needed to hear. I would stuff all the things they liked into their bag and send them home. My mom would have to go around collecting my toys and clothes back because, in my opinion, if they liked it, they could have it. My mom would say, "Hey, you just gave her a new dress with tags that you haven't even worn yet." But it didn't matter to me because they wanted it and my soul is Generosity. (That type of giving got me in trouble in my adult life, but that's another story.)

I AM Loyalty. If I'm on your team, I am going to be on your team no matter what. I left the Bay Area in 1996 and I'm still a 49er fan even through all the ups and the many downs. Once I'm on your team, I'm always on your team because I am Loyalty.

Then, my fifth one is **I AM Sensitivity**. I'm either crying, about to cry, or just got done crying. Those are the only three stages of my entire life. When I was younger, I thought, "Oh, I'm so weak. Why am I so emotional? Why does that bother me so much? Why can't I be like so and so? Nothing bothers her."

Everything bothered me. But now I realize that's because I Am Sensitivity. Now I can see it's my gift! I can walk into a room like a divining rod. I just know. I can tell you who to talk to and who not to talk to. I can stand up in a room and feel that energy. What I thought was my curse has been one of my greatest strengths.

So, when you go back in your mind and think about who you were as a little girl, ask yourself what she was like. It's okay if a couple of them are like mine. (I'll explain that a little later.) This might take some time for you to create your list because women have a hard time listing their greatness – don't worry. Take as long as you need and if you can't find five yet, don't worry you will.

If you say for example, I AM Caring – Caring is a trait that a human being has. What is underneath caring? Or why do you care? The answer simply is I AM Love and it translates as a human who cares. So, love is the soul quality underneath caring.

To help you a bit more, below are some examples of the 5 I AM statements of several women who have taken my workshops and groups over the years:

I AM Love. I AM Loyalty. I AM Compassion. I AM Wisdom. I AM Kindness.

I AM Healer. I AM Passion. I AM Connection. I AM Creativity. I AM Faith.

I AM Power. I AM Love. I AM Seeker. I AM Intelligence. I AM Light.

I AM Joy. I AM Peace. I AM Openness. I AM Creativity. I AM Connection.

I AM Magic. I AM Generosity. I AM Truth. I AM Intuition. I AM Seeker.

I AM Compassion. I AM Creativity. I AM Knowing. I AM Generosity. I AM Intelligence.

Problems happen when we forget the truth of who we are.

As every great teacher has said from Socrates and Plato to the New Thought Leaders of today, "The only reason you have any problems is that you have forgotten who you are." Now is your chance to sit for a moment with yourself. Think about your list and remember who you are. When you're ready, list your five I AM statements below.

Your I AMs

1. I AM_____

2. I AM_____

3. I AM_____

4. I AM_____

5. I AM_____

Congratulations! This is who you truly are! Not the things that have happened to you, not your personality, not your failures or mistakes but the divine magnificence that is your soul. This is where the work can really begin.

Read each statement to yourself. Introduce yourself to who your soul is now that you've given it the words to make it visible. Now, as you look at the list, you may begin to see that in order to be in a healthy, sustainable, and loving relationship with YOU, the people in your life must have the qualities on this list as well! That's right, look at it again...

In order to have a relationship with you that is healthy and works, the people in your life, your bosses, your mates, your friends, your family members must have these five qualities for it to work.

Stay with me here...

Here's the truth – you are simply looking for YOU everywhere! That's right, you heard me, you are looking for YOU everywhere. And when you see your soul mirrored back to you in the people across from you, you have found your people! Your people will marry you; your people will be good business partners; your people will be loyal and honest friends; your people will respect you and on and on!

I developed this tool because I personally had searched for so long. Even through all the esoteric studies, philosophy, theology, and psychology, I still couldn't grasp the one thing that I so deeply wanted to understand – that there's only one of us here. Uni-verse. One verse. I wanted to fully comprehend the concept so badly and live by it, but my mind couldn't understand it because I'm here and you're there. We are separate beings and physically apart so what do you mean there's only one of us here? Then it hit me. My I AMs!

When I see my own Kindness, Intelligence, Generosity, Loyalty and Sensitivity in the person across from me – I am going to be successful. They are me! Hence, "there's only one of us here – Universe – One Verse." And when you see what is on your list across from you, you will be successful too!

Did you notice how some of the I AM examples that I gave you earlier shared some of the same I AMs as mine? That's no coincidence! We find each other, our people, in all places; including the groups we join and the books we read.

Women spend too much time trying to make NOT their people, their people.

We are here to find our people, create a joyful life, accomplish our dreams, and manifest our definition of success and the only way to do that is to find the mirror of our best selves, which is your soul made visible through your I AMs.

Unfortunately, the problem women can often have is that we spend too much time trying to make NOT-our-people, our people. This is at the foundation of some of our biggest struggles and only leads to conflicts, high divorce rates, unfulfilling jobs, and friendships that don't last. We are suffering in situations that we don't need to stay in because we can't see ourselves in the people and situations around us. If that sounds familiar, be kind to yourself. You just never knew where to look or what to look for until now.

Success Story #1

Alicia is an actress who had moved from Florida to Los Angeles and was my assistant for a very long time.

Alicia and her sister were raised by a single mother who was the world's biggest Aerosmith fan. She would play Aerosmith all the time and take Alicia to concerts with her. Tragically, when Alicia was 13, her mother was killed by a valet driver who went through a crosswalk. Later, she lost her best friend to suicide at 16. And things didn't get any easier when she was diagnosed with stage three breast cancer at 23 years old.

But Alicia is an absolute rock star and after her own recovery, she wrote a book, created a movie, opened a non-profit and became an advocate for young women being allowed to get mammograms at any age.

So, when she started going back into her post-cancer acting career, she was cast in an American Idol commercial with thousands of other people. The three judges at the time were Jennifer Lopez, Randy Jackson, and... Steven Tyler from Aerosmith.

Only a few people were upgraded in the commercial to be a part of a smaller group that would walk behind each of the celebrity judges. And guess who gets picked to rock with Steven Tyler? Alicia! (This is when Alicia said a little prayer to her mother, "Okay mom, I can't believe you just did this to me!")

Normally, Alicia is the type of woman who is a huge extrovert but at this moment, she freaked out. Halfway through the day, she's frustrated and feeling so awkward that she can't even look at Steven. Finally, during their lunch break, she realizes, "Shit! I'm not being me, I am not being my I AMs."

Alicia went up to Steven and said, "Excuse me, Steven."

He turned around and she continued, "I'm sorry, I didn't introduce myself properly to you today. My name is Alicia."

"Oh, cool," he responded.

She said, "And I just want to say something. I know that I'm not a musician, but I want you to know that I meet you at your creativity."

And with that, Steven Tyler grabbed her hands, went nose to nose with her, and yelled, "I fucking love this!"

Then he kissed her on the forehead, and they rocked out together the rest of the day.

What happened at that moment was that they met at each other's souls. She had given him permission to be an actor and he had given her permission to be a rock star.

Now, that could have gone bad. He could have looked at her and said, "Okay," shrugged, and walked away. I asked her what if that would have happened and she said, "Then he wouldn't have been my people." Instead, he is her people and they aligned at the soul level once she showed up as her true self.

I can walk into some of the biggest boardrooms all over the country, with some of the toughest people. I know that if I walk in with my sword up, trying to match them, I will lose. Now if I go in as the Receiver, standing on a foundation of my I AMs (Kindness, Intelligence, Loyalty, Generosity, and Sensitivity), I can navigate the room truthfully and the people in that room will either be my people or they won't be.

However, if I'm in a situation with not-my-people, and I can't get out of it, I know my I AMs are something I need to make sure I'm standing in on behalf of myself. I make sure that I'm being kind to me. I make sure that I am being generous and loyal to me. Get what I'm saying?

This tool removes drama and victimhood from your life. I want to be clear that this is not a tool to make you judgmental of others. It is a tool to assist you in navigating from your soul.

Therefore, just because someone is "not-your-people" doesn't make them bad. They also have a list of I AMs, which show their magnificence. You're just not on their list and they are not on yours. And once you know someone is "not-your-people," the ego has nowhere to go with drama.

They may not get you, but they'll never rock you.

It used to take me 364 days a year to be able to see one of my brothers just once a year on Thanksgiving. I could not get along with that man. Black Friday for me was the first day of trying to get ready to see him next year.

He would walk into the house and the hairs on the back of my neck would stick up like a dog at a dog park. And, just like that, I would want to attack. I became instantly on the defense and felt I had to watch it, or I would start an argument just because he was breathing. It was that bad. Then I did this work. I looked at my list and realized (actually I was gobsmacked), "He's not on my list and, guess what, I'm not on his list either. He's just not-my-people."

Game over.

Every human being has a list of magnificence at their soul level. But the problem is, if they're not on your list, you're probably trying to force them on your list, which will not allow either one of you to participate in an authentic relationship.

My brother and I are never going to agree about life. We do not believe in the same things. He's never going to understand me, and I'm never going to understand him. It seems like we speak a different language. But the truth is that if I felt that way in his presence, he felt that way in mine. It doesn't mean either of us are bad, it means we are not on each other's lists and not each other's people. He might not get me, but he'll never rock me and my confidence in my I AMs. Knowing this changed everything.

I now have a relationship with my brother. Now, he calls and wishes me happy birthday. At Thanksgiving, we have conversations, not disagreements. I ask him to pass me the gravy, not the bottle of wine I once needed just to get through dinner with him. And women all over have confirmed that this tool has worked for them with their sibling relationships as well.

Once your soul is made visible you are empowered no matter what.

I have women who sit in my groups and say, "Okay, so here's the deal. I've done this exercise, and I've just realized my husband is not-my-people. But I don't want a divorce either."

When that happens, I say, "Okay. So, you're telling me you're clear, your mate is not-your-people."

"Yes, not-my-people."

"Okay, and you don't want a divorce?"

"No, I don't want a divorce. We have kids and I just don't feel like going through that."

Here's where I say, "Great."

Guess what? You have just empowered yourself. Now you're there by choice. He's never going to do anything you like. He's never going to be there for you. But he can also no longer disappoint you. You know why? He's not on your list. Now you have all the power. If you decide to stay, it's your choice. And if you decide to leave, it's also your choice. You can stop being a victim and live your life with the power of your own intention. Remembering that once your soul is made visible, you are empowered. No matter what the situation.

Here's the other part of this list. Not only are you looking for YOU everywhere and not only do you have to have every one of your I AMs present in a relationship, but you cannot teach these I AMs because they aren't things you learned yourself. Let that resonate for a moment.

You never learned any of these so you cannot teach them!
I hear women say things like, "Well, he's not very generous, but he had a really screwed-up childhood so I'm just going to give, give, give and he'll realize he's safe with me. When he does, he'll be more generous."

No, he won't. Remember, you came in this way. He didn't. Therefore, he's going to take, take, and take until he dumps you or you dump him. It's not going to work. I AM Generosity is on your list and you are trying to teach it to someone who just won't ever see it in the same way you do. They can't. It's not who they showed up on this earth as. They either have it or they don't, and he doesn't have it. I know this can be such a hard concept to grasp when we as women want to fix things and believe in someone's potential instead of allowing ourselves to truly see people for who they are.

You cannot teach people to be kind. You cannot teach people to be generous. You cannot teach people to have sensitivity for you. This is how important this list is. This is going to help you find your people. And if you have just woken up to the fact that you need to quit your job, great! Now you can find a job with your people. Or if you've realized you don't feel safe with your "friends," now you have the tools to find friendships with your people. Because here's the other great news. Ready?

If you don't feel good in their presence, they don't feel good in your presence either. That's just the way it goes. This is not a way for you to become better than anyone else. If you don't like them, they don't like you. If you don't like spending time with them, they don't like spending time with you either.

And what anyone else's list looks like, doesn't matter. Focus on finding your I AMs in others, not yourself in someone else's list. I want you to read that again, this is VERY important.
Focus on finding your I AMs in others, not yourself on someone else's list.

When I meet someone, the only question I have is, "Can I see my Kindness in them? Can I see my Generosity in them?" Not, "I wonder what's on their list and can I see myself on it." That's their job. For instance, my husband's first I AM is "I AM Creativity." As you know, I AM Creativity is not on my list, but he sees his

Creativity in me, so I am his people. He does not have Loyalty on his list, but I can see my Loyalty in him. The worst thing you can do is start comparing your list to anyone else's because when you do, you are stepping away from who you are at your soul level and filtering it through the lens of someone else. I want to stress to you that this does not mean we have the same personality. These are tools for soul alignment not personality alignment. When it comes to personality, my husband and I are polar opposites but we meet at our I AMs.

This list is for you and you alone, and it doesn't matter what is on anyone else's list. Remember that. What this tool does is to make YOUR soul visible so that they can see it too. This creates an authentic connection to your people. A necessary connection to accomplish your dreams.

You may be wondering what if I can see that somebody has four out of my five? Okay, great. Which one of these would you like to live without? Your Intelligence? Your Generosity? Your Truth? Your Creativity? Would you like to live without Love? How's that one for you? What would you decide you could live without?

You can't do it! (Or, at least not for long and be happy.)

Why is that? Because remember, this is Source that is coming through you. If they're missing one, that's the one that will be what takes the relationship down eventually. It may be days, months or even years from now. But eventually, you will find that you have to leave the situation because you cannot show up there fully.

When you walk into a room, your I AMs walk in with you. Our I AMs are how we meet each other. They are your power and how you need to show up in the world. If you are Intelligence and you walk into a room only to defer to someone else when you know better, you're at a disadvantage and so is the room. However, if you stand solid with your soul visible and your Intelligence shining bright, that is how you empower a room.

Your I AMs empower you to meet others at your soul instead of your personality.

Knowing your I AMs levels the playing field and it becomes about meeting people at your soul instead of at your personality.

In one of my workshops, I had a woman who was a first-time winning female director at Sundance, and-I said to her, "Okay, so give me one of your I AMs."

"I Am a Director," she says.

"You are? Cool. You've got Scorsese on your left, and you've got Spielberg on your right, are you a director now?"

"Well, I'm just starting. I'm not like them but I'm doing pretty well..."

I said, "Whoa, Whoa, you got all defensive and weird on me. So, now let's take a step back. You're a director. What's underneath directing for you?"

"Creativity," she said.

"Great. Spielberg's on your right and he says to you, 'Hey, I Am Creativity,' what would you say?"

"Me, too."

Boom. See, we meet at our souls. Our problems begin when we get human and we start comparing ourselves to each other. Instead, we need to understand that the mirror of our souls matching each other is the magic that fosters our accomplishments. Your I AMs take the human component and breaks it down to the soul level. And that's the embodiment of Power.

Life may have gotten hard and unfair, and I know some of you reading this have had to go through loss, pain, and abuse. I understand. I truly get that. But these are the tools to get past your story, to go to the truth, to return to your soul, where you are safer than anywhere else you could be.

Success Story #2

A woman in one group told us that after recognizing her I AMs, she called her manager at work the next day. In her words, she "hated her life" because of a particular conflict she had been having with her manager, which had been causing her to feel powerless in her job.

After going over her I AMs, she realized that she had been telling herself these stories around the issue, "Oh, she hates me. I hate her." But now she realized that what she had been telling herself might not have even been true.

She looked at her I AMs, saw I AM Power, and knew then that she had the power to change the situation. She told the group that her manager had been in shock that she had even reached out. The manager told her, "I am so happy that you reached out to me. I know it took so much courage for you to pick up the phone and call me."

"It's the craziest thing," she said about the conversation.

"That one phone call changed everything."

She hadn't been operating from "I AM Power" at her soul level and was instead allowing herself to be disempowered every day. But as soon as she had stepped into her first I AM, the manager had recognized it and acknowledged the courage it had taken for her to call. That was all that was needed to put them on an even playing field and begin repairing the situation.

After having the conversation with her manager and standing in her I AMs, she no longer hated going to work. The people around her had even taken notice and told her how different she was now.

Isn't that interesting? The woman in the previous story was not being her true self so, of course, she couldn't navigate her work situation with ease. However, once she began to act with her soul (instead of her personality), everyone noticed a difference – including her!

Again, women waste so much time trying to make not-their-people and make them their people when we really can't, no matter how hard we try. They're not any less than us. It's like music. We just don't play the same note. A note of B flat cannot play a note of E sharp. It doesn't even try; it can only play its own note.

Using this tool to transform relationships, the path to accomplishing your dreams will become more effortless. There may be a realignment with the people in your life that you feel resistance with. That's okay. With this new awareness, you no longer have to be at war with them about it. Instead, you now understand that they also have their own list of magnificence. You're just not on it.

You will begin to shed the relationships that feel like obligations; especially those friendships that use up your precious energy and take you down. I don't care if you guys grew up together or have known each other since high school, the truth is she doesn't like you either and this relationship is not easy for either of you.

Once you are really living your truth and standing in your I AMs, you'll stop attracting not-your-people because they won't even be on your radar. You'll quickly realize, "Oh yeah, not-my-people. I'm not working with that person." You'll start to have so much more power and will begin to notice the abundance of your people coming to work with you.

From now on, put your I AMs in front of you. Take every step from that I AM place. Treat yourself with the magnificence that you are.

That is God. That is Source. That is Power.

Tools in Motion

1. Review your I AM list daily. Remind yourself of the truth of who you are, not your circumstance.

2. Place your list on the wallpaper of your phone to see it all day. Also, place them on notes in different places like your computer screen, bathroom mirror etc.

3. Each time you are about to get on a call, send a written correspondence, or go into a meeting situation, ask yourself to do it from the list of who you are – notice the outcomes and practice, practice, practice.

4, Be aware of "not-your-people" and use your I AMs to navigate the situations. Do not use this to judge others, use it to empower yourself.

Good to Know

1. I AM is your connection to greatness.

2. Problems happen when we forget the truth of who we are.

3. Women spend too much time trying to make NOT their people, their people.

4. They may not get you, but they'll never rock you.

5. Once your soul is made visible you are empowered no matter what.

6. Your I AMs empower you to meet others at your soul instead of your personality.

Continuing the Conversation

For a more in-depth understanding of this tool, please join me for a video which will assist you in creating and accessing your I AMs.

http://www.thequinnessentials.com/IAM/

or scan QR code

Chapter III

LISTEN

Listening is advanced Receiving.

Welcome to Tool Number Three, **LISTEN**.

Listening is truly a form of advanced receiving from which you can receive the information necessary to navigate your life with strength and power. This is why we MUST Listen! Everything we need to know can be found within us once we stop the chatter of what we think and truly listen to what we know. While we **hear** through our ears, we receive information fully when we **listen** from the center of our being, which resides in the middle of our chest. (Sometimes referred to as our Heart Center.) Listening from this center, we can receive all the answers we need.

Much like women can have a hard time receiving (I know you may still be digesting that chapter), we as women can also have a hard time listening. This is because we typically have a habit of thinking ahead while others are still talking. We are so busy planning our comebacks in order to get what we want out of the conversation that we often miss hearing the information we asked for. I know this is a habit we've developed out of perceived need because we've been used to not getting what we want and not feeling heard.

We've also learned not to listen as an act of self-protection. For those of us who grew up with a steady diet of verbal abuse, we learned how to shut off our listening because we didn't want to hear certain things. But hearing and listening are two totally different actions.

One of the most frustrating things in the world is not being heard. But, when you're busy planning what you're going to say while the other person is still talking, you're not listening to them either. Trust me, people know when you're not listening to them.

Has anyone ever said to you, "You're not listening to me!"? Personally, I can answer "yes" to that question. There may seem to be a lot of reasons we don't listen in addition to the ones I listed, but one of the biggest reasons is it has simply become a habit. A habit that we must work hard to break so we can navigate our lives more powerfully.

In this chapter, we're going to talk about the necessity of breaking that habit in relation to accomplishing your dreams. I'm also going to share with you how to listen in two very important ways: Part One – Listening to Others and Part Two – Listening to Ourselves.

Listening Part One

"I knew that!"

First, let's talk about listening to others.

In the world, you must listen to what people are telling you versus listening with the potential of what you want to hear. All too often, women listen with potential.

I get it. We want it to be a certain way so much that we hear how things could be instead of fully hearing what the other person across from us is actually saying. This is especially true in dating. This is the form of listening that almost always leads to misunderstandings.

For example, maybe you're with a man, and he's almost 50 and he's never been married or never lived with anyone. You want a commitment. You want to get married. You want to have a family. You're going out with this guy, and you ask him, "So, why haven't you ever gotten married before?"

"Well, I haven't really ever met the right one."

I'm going to tell you the truth.

Yes, he has.

Several times.

This one doesn't commit.

But you knew that already, didn't you? Think about it. THIS IS EXACTLY WHY YOU'RE ASKING HIM THOSE QUESTIONS.

You're interrogating him because at your center, deep down, in the middle of your chest, you already know that this is not the father of your children. You know that this is not going to happen for you with him. No matter how hard you want it to be or how tired of looking you are, this isn't it.

Same rules apply when you're dating a woman. If she's never committed, she's 48, still lives with her mom, and admittedly has no friends – **slam on those brakes**. Something's wrong. Ask more of those questions that your center is telling you to ask and make sure to really invest the time listening to what she is telling you (not what you're hoping for) before getting into a relationship with her.

If a relationship is what you want, don't be with someone who doesn't commit. As I like to tell my friends, "Red isn't a pretty color when it comes in the form of a flag." Women ignore red flags and don't listen when, in the end, they will inevitably say they knew something wasn't right from the beginning.

What are some of the phrases women say more frequently than any other?

"I knew that!"
"I knew they weren't going to pay me back."
"I knew she was not really my friend."
"I knew that boss was never going to promote me."
"I knew they were cheating."
"I knew, I knew, I knew, I knew."

You know why we know? Because besides being fabulous, we have this internal navigation system within us that tells us the truth every minute of every day. How fantastic is that?! You really do know all the answers because you are a receiver, and this type of listening is clearly advanced receiving.

We simply do not listen. The irony is that women don't like to be told what to do even if it's by ourselves. We stopped listening to ourselves because we thought that we were the cause of the problems. We judge ourselves for being wrong or making bad decisions. But, the majority of the time, the cause of making past mistakes comes from not listening to our inner guidance and, instead, looking for answers outside of ourselves.

Or here's what else we do. We take it in (receive the guidance), listen and then we bring it up between our ears for review. And then we begin to deliberate, doubt, judge and become so confused that we decide to call up all our friends and ask them. We ask other people's opinions about our lives, we follow someone else's advice but when things don't work out, what do we so often say? "Damn, I knew what to do from the beginning. I just didn't listen."

Success Story #1

I had a woman in one of my workshops who said that her three

accomplishments were: 1. She wanted to get married. 2. She wanted to get married. And 3. She wanted to get married.

It was after our class on "Listening" that she came back and shared with us that she had an epiphany. She had gone on a date with someone who was perfect on paper. And she had finally listened...

This woman had two little chihuahuas. They were her only family in Los Angeles and she adored them. She would even dress them up in outfits that matched her own. She loved them so much that she would lay on her pillow at night and the dogs would sleep in her long wavy hair like in a Disney movie.

On her date, she asked him if he liked dogs and he said, "Not really, I don't really get it."

She had heard that before from other men and always thought, "Well, he just hasn't met mine yet." But this time she really heard it for the first time in her life. She thought to herself, "Okay. I'm finishing this dinner and then I'm going home to my dogs."

She finished that meal and never saw him again because she had finally listened. She knew this guy wasn't going to fall in love with her dogs. He doesn't like dogs. And dogs are the most important thing to her.

Here's what else happened... While listening to herself, she also heard that she needed to move back home to Philadelphia. She listened, got a big job back East and because she loves dogs *as much as she does, she volunteered on the weekends at a dog shelter. And that is where she met a lawyer who also donated his time at the dog shelter.*

Guess what? They are now married with three dogs.

Do you see how in the above story she finally listened to what was really being said? She didn't listen with potential and try to make it any different than it was. She avoided being disappointed (again) and listened right from the start realizing the path to breaking her habit of not listening had begun.

Not listening is a habit that you can break.

The same is true in our careers. Let's say you're sitting across from somebody and you've gotten yourself in a desperate situation where you need work. You're in an interview for a job, and the person across from you says, "Well, we work hard, we make a lot of money, but we don't have lives..." You take the job, and then you wonder why they're calling you on a Sunday for work. You're now upset because it's your day off.

Wait a minute... Don't you remember? They told you in the interview, "We don't have lives." You just weren't listening. Instead, you attached so much meaning to the phrase "We make a lot of money" that you completely bypassed the "We don't have lives."

I've had so many people tell me that after taking my course, they finally started listening in interviews. For example, if you're a single mother and you're raising a family on your own, and the boss tells you that you won't have a life if you work there, ask yourself, how's that supposed to work for you?

If you take that job out of desperation, you know that in less than 30 days you'll have to quit because – Murphy's Law – your child will get sick at school and you're going to have to leave work and go to school in the middle of your workday to pick them up.

Just as we need to break the habit of thinking while someone is talking, we need to relearn how to listen. How to start listening begins with awareness and the act of being present. A lot of people have a hard time being present. I understand how difficult it can be. Especially if you want to get your way. But in order to interrupt your habit of not listening, you must start with awareness of the present moment. When you are present, you don't miss the vital information in a situation, which will then help you to navigate things in your life more effortlessly. (Even if you don't like what you are hearing.) Personally, I like to tell myself, "Andrea – be here now." It helps to bring me back into the moment and to focus on what the person is truly saying to me.

A way to keep yourself in check is to repeat what people say back to them. This will confirm that what you heard was really being said. This is a powerful exercise that not only allows you to hear it again as you say it out loud but, very importantly, it gives the person you are speaking to the chance to also hear what they said. Repeating it back also requires that you listen and keeps you accountable for being present in the conversation.

When people say something to me, I'll reply with, "Okay, so here's what I'm hearing," and then repeat back what I've heard from them. Sometimes they'll say to me, "Yeah, that's what I said." Or, other times, they'll say, "No, that's not what I said. What I said was ..."

Isn't that interesting? Just because you heard it, doesn't mean that's what they said! When you repeat it back and give the other person the opportunity to confirm or clarify, everything becomes so much clearer during the conversation. Listening to others not only allows you to be guided to make decisions based on clarity, but it also gives the person you are speaking with a form of respect and lessens miscommunications. And who doesn't want that?

Now that we discussed listening to others it is time for the part of this chapter on listening to yourself.

Listening Part Two

To accomplish your dreams, you must be able to listen to yourself.

YOU MUST LISTEN TO YOUR OWN INNER VOICE! You have spent far more time not listening to her (your inner you) than you have spent listening to her. Why? Because you think she couldn't possibly know what's good for you – you think she's gotten you into all those messes, remember?

Let me tell you this – She is always right. She always has been. And she always will be. You just don't want to hear it. We don't like to be told what to do, especially if it's something that doesn't feel good or is something we don't want to hear. Even if it's coming from within ourselves. But, to accomplish your dreams, you must develop a relationship of self-trust so that you are able to listen to yourself.

I know this is easier said than done. But, since I spent a lot of my life cleaning up messes from not listening to my inner guidance, I developed this next process to not only listen to myself but to gain clarity in my life.

The way you're going to start listening to yourself is by getting clear about your **Requirements**.

For example, let's imagine you were going to take a class at a university. What's the first thing you must look at before signing up? **The Requirements.** Once you know what the course requires, you have the power of being able to make a knowledgeable choice; you know if you fulfill the requirements, you can take the class. If you don't have them, you will have to take another class or you can decide, based on the requirements, not to take the class at all. But there is absolutely no noise or wiggle room around what the requirements are to take the class or not. You must have that type of certainty, which comes by listening to yourself. It's not about finding out what you "need" or what you "demand"; it's about what you require.

Need, however, is very different from a requirement. Women don't know what they require but typically know exactly what they need. But when women are in need, we are in the vibration of lack, and it takes so much energy just to get us back up to our baseline of feeling empowered and whole. Let me say this again...When you need something, you are in lack. (You don't have it and someone or something else has the power over you in that situation). It feels horrible to feel disempowered and be in a place where you "need" something from someone. I have had many experiences like this in my life and I have a horrible visceral reaction to that word.

Think about these sentences and how they feel as you read them:

"I need you to be nice to me."
"I need you to pay me more money."
"I need you to stop this behavior."
"I need you to listen to me."

Then, what happens when we don't get what we need? We start becoming angry, which causes us to be demanding:

"I demand you speak to me with respect."
"I demand that you pay me more money."
"I demand you keep your agreement."
"I demand you be kind to my family."

IT'S THE SAME BURRITO, DIFFERENT SALSA. You're just angry this time because you're still in need and you're still in lack. Need and demand are different sides of the same coin. They are filled with disempowered emotion and lack. Requirements are not emotional or demanding, they are solid and powerful.

A requirement is something that can never change.

Now, let's talk more about your **requirements**. A requirement is something that can never change. I know that's a BIG statement. That's because your requirements come from your core and are what aligns you so that you can function at the highest level. No matter the changes that life may bring your way, what aligns you with your core doesn't change. Knowing your requirements means knowing who you are and where you stand no matter what happens. How empowering is that? VERY!

The only way to develop your requirements is by sitting and listening to yourself as you begin to create them. This is not only an empowering exercise, it is a courageous one. You will see that it takes courage to stand in your requirements.

It takes courage to ask yourself questions like, Do you know what you're going to require from situations in your life? How about from your boss? From your friends? From your love relationship? Or do you default back to need?

Do you remember I told you about my husband, Chris? When I realized that it was going to be my third marriage, I figured I'd better get it together because there was a common denominator... And that common denominator was me. I knew from my past track record that I had to figure out what my requirements for my relationship was going to be. So, I sat with myself and looked at who I really was and began to listen. Even if I didn't like what I heard from myself, I still listened with the intention of healing and creating a trusting relationship with my inner voice. It was one of the hardest things I ever had to do.

At first, I asked myself, What were the most important things to me in a relationship? What were the things I tried to "fix" or wasn't honest about before so that I could have a successful and sustainable union now? What were the issues that caused my relationships to blow up in the past?

When you are figuring out your requirements, it is not a list of the things you want – it is the things that are non-negotiable. Non-negotiables are what you are very sure you cannot live with, as well as the things you know you cannot live without. As a woman, I always thought I could change things or adapt to my partner. But what I discovered is that we all have non-negotiable, core requirements that need to be met. When we don't have them fulfilled, we can't have successful relationships.

I'd like to share with you here what my personal requirements for a love relationship are so that you can see how I created them. Later in the chapter, I'm going to give you the opportunity to take some time, listen to yourself, and create your own personal requirement list.

Andrea's Requirements

Number One: I require that my husband doesn't yell at me. Ever. As much as I loved him, my father was a rageaholic who was either angry, about to get angry, or just got over being angry. Remember, I mentioned that "I AM Sensitivity?" Well, I don't do yelling. During my entire childhood because I AM Sensitivity, I was jumpy and anxious. When I had to defend myself, I would become aggressive, and with my "I AM Kind," that was no bueno because that was not really me. When someone yells at me, it triggers things in me that turns me into somebody I don't like and that I can't respect.

So, when we were dating and it came time to talk to my husband about my requirements, I told him, "I'm going to require that you don't yell at me. And you will want to because it's me. But here's the deal. You can get up and leave instead of yelling at me, and I won't follow you and egg you on. But I can't be yelled at. That's for sure. That's my requirement." He took in what I was requiring, and he agreed that he was grateful that I was so clear in my communication with him.

After 20 years of marriage, I can tell you that my husband has never yelled at me. Not once. And I have deserved it so many times. Instead, I just sit still because I know he's trying to calm down, so he doesn't yell at me. It takes a lot of restraint from both of us, but I understand what is at stake for me even in a heated disagreement.

Because it's my requirement, it cannot be any other way.

Number Two: I require that he has a job.

Personally, I have a problem within a relationship if I am working and my partner isn't. (That is not true for many women, but it is true for me.) Every relationship is different, but I had to be honest with myself about my feelings. My requirement is that if I work, you work! I know if he doesn't, I will lose respect for him immediately. And what's not fair to my husband is I have no problem with other men not working in other relationships. I totally get their situation but in my own relationship, it will not work for me. (I never said I was perfect; I just know myself.) My husband loves to tease me and asks what would happen if we won at a *scratch and win lottery* ticket. I tell him that if we *scratch and win*, I will still ask him to work, because we need to contribute to society. I'm not saying he must go out there and earn money, but he has to put energy into the world through service. My husband is a fantastic gourmet chef. So, if we *scratch and win*, I will want him to be down at the mission donating his time and cooking for the homeless.

I must be participating in the world constantly. If he was the kind of guy who wanted to retire to Montana when he's older and get deck-butt while he fishes, I wouldn't be his girl because I don't want to retire. Ever. And if God blesses me with health and longevity, I'm going to be the hottest 80-year-old volunteer tour guide at the zoo telling everyone to look at the new baby cubs.

I was very honest and upfront about how important working and volunteering is to me and he agreed to my requirement.

Number Three: I require that he has his own relationship with my family and must be a participating member who contributes, separate from me to my family.

And that means he's not going to just visit them three times a year, lay on the couch, eat free on the holidays, and then leave. That's not going to work for me because I'm going to contribute to his family too.

My family is a solid tribe, and you must have a relationship with them. My parents, my aunts and uncles and all the family members... They will know everything about you. They are involved in every aspect of my life. The worst thing you can ever do in a relationship with me is say, "Don't tell your mom." It's never going to happen. You have an upset stomach? She knows. She's probably already sent a remedy. It's just the way it is.

And it has been from his own deep, personal, love for my family that Chris has been an integral part of my beloved tribe. At the end of my father's life, when we all took turns taking care of my dad, my husband had just as much time as my own brothers, and sometimes even more.

How did I come up with my **Three Requirements?** I had listened to myself, and I knew that to be in a loving relationship that would work for me, I had to require those three things of my mate – **you don't yell at me, you have a job, and you become an active participant in my family.**

Those three requirements are the non-negotiables that I have in my life. Those are the things that always caused my previous relationships to end. So, I had to do some deep diving to get real with myself so I could navigate a relationship and have it last. By being honest with Chris regarding my requirements and listening to my own voice, I had a road map for success in a relationship that I never had before.

It was very scary for me to have requirements in the beginning, knowing that I would have to walk away from a man I was dating, but if I didn't have my requirements communicated to him, then I had the chance of having another relationship fail.

*However, ladies, there is a 'duh' list. If you have to require "they will not hit me," or "they will not use my social security number without my permission," or "they will not hit on my friends," those are on the 'duh' list. You shouldn't even have to require those things. If you feel you do, I already can tell you they are not-your-people.

People tell you everything if you listen!

Let's say you're about to start a relationship, and you ask yourself, "What are you going to require from this relationship?" But your answer is that you don't know. Well, I ask you this: If you don't know, how are they supposed to know?

This also applies to every area of your life. You must also have requirements for your jobs. You must be transparent with your employers, clients, and employees. And you must listen to yourself first to do so.

For example, let's say you're a single mom and you go to an interview. Wouldn't it be empowering to know what you will require from your employers and then to be able to articulate it to them? How empowering is it to let them know what your requirements are regarding your family and obligations while displaying confidence that you would be an amazing asset to their company? (I love powerful women!) Asking questions like, "What is your policy on supporting single parents?" is a way to take the interview back into your own hands and find out if it's the right job for you and your family. Can you see now how listening to yourself and discovering what you require are imperative to your personal empowerment and transformation?

Life shows up in different ways, but you've got to know yourself well enough so you're ready for it when it does. Differentiating requirements from needs and demands is fundamentally important as well. Now you can start telling people what you're going to require, stepping away from the lower vibration of need and into the higher vibration of empowerment. Knowing your requirements doesn't limit you or your options. Instead, listening and knowing what you require helps you to release what does not serve you, so when the opportunities do come your way, you are able to fully recognize and embrace them.

Success Story #2

There's a wonderful woman in our community who is a well-known stand-up comedian. After she took my workshop, she began to listen to what people were really telling her.

At the time, she was with one of the top comedy managers in the business. Everybody who's anybody has this guy as their manager. But he never really cared about what she did, and he never went to any of her shows. And you can imagine that as a result, she never felt fully supported.

Anyone who knows her is clear that her family and her kids are her life. In order to be able to perform at night, she would have to have her little babies sleeping out in the car in the parking lot and go back and forth to check on them. This is what it was like for her as a single mother working in the comedy world.

After this class, when she looked at her list of her I AMs and what she knew she required by listening to herself, she not only saw that he wasn't her people, but she also heard loudly that she needed to find someone else to represent her. Coming to that realization, she finally said, "Enough. I can't do this anymore. I'm going to go find a manager that I feel supported with" and left him.

Before she went to her initial interview with another manager, she made sure she had her I AMs and her list of requirements. During her meeting, before she could even start to list what she wanted, he asked her about her kids. When she told him she had two, he instantly said, "That must be hard." And continued to say how he and his wife felt that family should always come first.

As they spoke more, she noticed her I AMs coming from him, and he addressed her requirements without her even mentioning them.

Then he said to her, "By the way, I'd love to come to one of your shows. In fact, if I represent you, I'll be at all your shows. And, if at any time, you need a babysitter, my wife will be happy to help and take care of the kids while you work."

She had found her people by knowing what she required and by listening. She signed with him, and her career took off. Because, when you listen, you see that people are telling you everything you need to know.

Ladies, they are telling you everything! But are you listening? Are you truly – I mean really and truly – listening to what they're saying? Or are you hearing from your mind and turning it into what you want them to say so it'll be the way you want it to be?

If so, how has that been working for you? I can tell you it doesn't, and what happens instead is that we get disappointed time and time again.

Knowing your requirements is a form of self-respect.

You will notice that people will begin to feel safer with you because they know what you require from them. When a person has respect enough for themselves to be deeply connected to their self-listening, there is a palpable power that emanates from them that others can see.

Women have told me they fear that taking this type of stand with solid requirements will result in people thinking they are a bitch. I always say, "You can never be a bitch when you know what you require; you become a bitch when you don't receive your requirements!" (Aren't we always the angriest when we didn't listen to what we knew in the first place?)

Another huge question I ask women is, "Do you know what you require from yourself?" That is a huge revelation. What are you going to require from yourself as a lover, as a friend, as an employee? Do you know? If you don't, then I recommend listening to yourself and becoming accountable to YOU.

You can't take those jobs that make you feel bad. You can't date those people who aren't going to work out for you. And you can't hang out with those friends who don't make you feel safe. Now you know that when you "Listen," you'll know those answers and begin to see situations and people for who they are – not who or what you want them to be.

From now on, I want you to practice silencing your mind. Listen from your center to what is being said by others as well as yourself. Know your requirements. This form of self-respect makes you the most solid woman in the room. And people want to be around solid women because they know where they stand.

For sure, these are power tools to use while on the road to accomplishing your dreams!

Tools in Motion

1. Practice repeating back to people what you think you heard them say. Be open to it being different than what you thought!

2. Thank people for communicating even if you don't like what was said to acknowledge you heard them.

3. Use a "listen and respond" exercise. As soon as you hear something in your center, act on it. For example, you are on the highway, and something in you says, "Take the exit," just do it – don't think "Oh well, I will just sit here in traffic; I am almost home." OR when you hear within yourself to not eat at a certain establishment – Don't! Just go to a place that might be farther away but listen to your first instincts. (We must practice this

because we are used to doubting ourselves.)

4. Sit with a paper and pen (preferably outside with no device) and begin to list 3 or 4 requirements in an area of your life that you are working on. Maybe it's a relationship or job? (This will be hard in the beginning but will become more and more clear as you work through them.)

Good to Know

1. I knew that!

2. Not listening is a habit you can break.

3. To accomplish your dreams, you must be able to listen to yourself.

4. A requirement is something that can never change.

5. People tell you everything if you listen.

6. Knowing your requirements is a form of self-respect.

Continuing the Conversation

To further your understanding of the importance of listening and creating your requirements, join me for this video.

http://www.thequinnessentials.com/listen/

or scan QR code

Chapter IV

SELF-ACCEPTANCE

***True power is the complete acceptance of your
magnificence.***

As we move into Tool Number Four, **Self-Acceptance**, I wanted to take a moment to remind you that one of the biggest keys to navigating the tools in your Quinn Essentials Toolkit is that they work – if you use them.

I know that these tools are not easy!

You will have to face a lot of the stuff that you don't want to face. But I promise you, once you start facing them, you'll realize how much power you have over them and, from that point on, it just gets easier and easier.

You may be finding that you haven't talked to yourself like this in a long time, if ever. Or maybe you haven't ever really asked yourself who you are at the soul level, let alone what you would like to receive. Trust me, I get it. And I know these can be hard conversations that you're not used to having with yourself.

That's okay. It's normal to find this hard.

I try to make it light when I am sharing these tools, but they are very serious to me. When we are receiving new information or old information in a new way, it is important to share it with levity because isn't life serious enough? I believe that when you make yourself the priority, inside and out, your life can't help but start working. Or, at the very least, we can get really clear on what isn't working, and then go back into our Toolkit to select the right tool that will shift everything for you so it does work.

For me, having these 9 tools is why teaching my workshops have been so important and why I have decided to write this book. I know how essential it is for women to begin to utilize these tools to empower themselves and accomplish the things they desire in their lives.

Self-Acceptance is the last tool that you're going to work on from the inside and is a key component to the rediscovery of your personal empowerment.

Here's where I'm magnificent, and I can fully accept it.

Self-Acceptance is the tool I spoke about in Chapter Two that I would cover later around your "humanness." While your I AMs are your soul made visible – the foundation you walk on – your Self-Acceptance is your "humanness" that separates you and what makes you unique as a human.

Most of the time people define Self-Acceptance as "Here's where I'm good. Here's where I'm bad. I just have to love the whole package." (Who can do that, honestly??)

In this book, Self-Acceptance is "Here's where I'm magnificent and I can fully accept it."

We all know the things we don't know how to do, especially as women. We are hard on ourselves and have that everlasting list of the things we need to fix before we can have happiness or success. We keep a running inventory of all the tasks to work on to "better" ourselves versus making a list of our talents and gifts. We have set that bar so high out of self-punishment, and we will never attain it.

Self-Acceptance is pure acceptance of your gifts and what you are good at. It is your talents. It is the act of honoring yourself. If one of your I AMs is "I AM Creativity," your Self-Acceptance is "I can accept that I'm a great songwriter." And then can you see your song writing is being supported by your I AM Creativity?

By using this tool, you will begin moving in the direction of truly seeing what is "right" with you and where your particular excellence lives. Here's the truth, "**What's wrong with you is not your job to fix and none of your business**." Your job is to figure out what's right with you and ask how you can get better at that. The expansion of your gifts and talents is not only easier to focus on, but it can also get you much further than trying to develop skills that just don't come naturally. Self-Acceptance is the path to your inner knowledge and the secret to an effortless life. Do you see now how much more powerful you are in moving forward now from this place?

Think of all the energy you've spent trying to fix something that you think is broken about you. It's a waste of time. Time is finite and we only have so much time in our days and in our lives. Invest your time in expanding what you are good at because those are the breadcrumbs to follow on the path to your accomplishments.

Stop trying to fix her! There's nothing wrong with her! This tool is about not only interrupting that behavior but, most importantly, shifting our perspective to embrace all that we DO know how to create and honor the talents within ourselves.

Everything you're good at is a gift.

Ask yourself: Where is it that you are magnificent? Where do you rock? What are your gifts? (Don't tell me your mind just went blank.)

I believe that Source, the Universe or God, gives you these gifts. That's what I like to call my diamond ring. But some of you keep your diamond ring in the drawer. Some of you think it's too small and are in judgment of it.

Take it out of the drawer, let it sparkle and know that you are wonderful! You came in this way and everything you're good at is a gift. The issue is that you are in judgment of your talents, believing somehow they are not good enough.

Let's say, you came in with a beautiful voice. Not everyone came in with a beautiful voice. That's a gift. Or, let's say, you have this incredible ability with numbers. Not everybody's great with numbers. Guess what... That's a gift. Your job is to get better at whatever gift you were given and to now see how all those attempts at fixing what you're not good at are a waste of time, which takes you away from supporting and honoring your own diamond ring.

Your job now is to figure out an expansion plan for your gifts and talents. Doesn't that sound nice? (Go ahead and exhale, things just got easier.)

In this next part, I am going to give examples of things I am not good at for learning purposes only. These will be stories from my life to illustrate the contrast between non-Acceptance and Self-Acceptance. I want to be clear that I never focus on where I am not good at something. I constantly practice the tool of Self-Acceptance.

Lady Shame feels real, but it's just an illusion.

Before I realized my own magnificence, I thought I had to be good at everything. I had a lot of "Lady Shame" when it came to all the things I was not good at. Lady Shame is a term created by the brilliant writer Rita Merson to describe the shame women feel by the social and cultural standards put on them whereby we experience negative evaluation of self. When you have that kind of shame, it feels so real everywhere – even in your body, but it is an illusion of the ego and simply fear. One of my shameful big secrets is that I cannot cook. Not at all. I mean I can't even get oatmeal and toast to come out at the same time. I have shiny object syndrome and I forget it's even on the stove. I don't know how people do that.

I come from an amazing line of chefs and even married one. It doesn't matter. No matter how hard I try, I can't. It's just not in my gift basket. When I was dating, I was so embarrassed by my inability to cook that one of my girlfriends would come over, cook for my date, and then leave out the back door. Later, while he 'oooh'ed and 'ahhh'ed over the meal, I would say that I prepared it. That's how deeply ashamed I was.

So now here's where I'm excellent, I may not like to cook but I love to eat. Food is just something I know.

I'm so good at eating, I can taste something and ask, "Is there a clove in there?" They'll say, "There's no way you tasted that! It was a dash." But I can and I do because one of my gifts is being a self-proclaimed food sommelier. I love food and eating. So, while I may not understand the process of how it got on my plate, I know exactly what ingredients it took to get there. That is my superpower.

Now, instead of being embarrassed that I don't cook, I accept my deep love for food and am currently writing a cookbook titled, *Nine Spanish Sisters – a Tribute of Love and Family.*

My mother and her eight sisters are incredible cooks. And so, I am writing a cookbook of their recipes, my relationship with each one of my aunts and all the recipes I want you guys to make so I can come over and eat it!

To do that, I had to know where I'm already magnificent.

Most people won't allow themselves to write a cookbook if they don't cook. They're too worried about what people think. I'm not worried about what people think because I know the recipes are amazing.

Notice how I didn't say that I'd make them for you. I own my gifts and will be honest about who I am. At the start of the cookbook, I will tell you, "I do not know how to cook." Why? Because I'm not embarrassed by it anymore. That shame is just an illusion blinding us to where we are magnificent – don't forget that.

We hide things out of embarrassment. But the truth is I know what I'm good at. And, if you judge me for something that I'm not good at, then you're just not-my-people. (See how easy that was?)

Another example is if I go to an event and people want to talk about stocks, I couldn't care less. NASDAQ is it a Q or a K? I don't even know how to spell it! And who is Dow Jones? I don't know who he is, and I'm not interested.

I used to stand there and think that maybe I should educate myself because I was embarrassed about not knowing or caring about stocks. Not anymore. If I don't resonate with conversations about the stock market, it doesn't mean I am not intelligent. It means I'm not interested.

However, I am interested in taking care of my money, so that's what stockbrokers are for. And instead of trying to learn something I'm not good at and don't want to learn, I spend that time being magnificent in what it is I do. Because when I do that, I can hire the right people who are magnificent in what they do and can take care of my money for me. It's a win, win.

If you're going to be successful, you must acknowledge your gifts.

I'm not afraid to say that I don't understand stocks or that I'm never going to cook for you guys, EVER. That's Self-Acceptance. But, to do that, I must stand solidly in my Self-Acceptance. Again, if you're going to be successful, you have got to know where you're magnificent and stop trying to fix what you think is broken about you. When you start to do that, you will stop wasting your precious time and energy.

As an example, if you want to expand your business, think "Okay, what's one thing I am good at?" Figure out how to apply that to the first step of expansion. If you say to yourself, "I am good at organizing," then apply your organizational skills to your business and watch things begin to move in a more successful direction.

As you started this book, I asked you to write down the three things you want to accomplish. Now, at the end of this chapter, I want you to ask yourself where are you magnificent, talented, or gifted in areas that relate to what you want to accomplish already?

For example, if you want to find love and get married, where are you already lovable? Where are you already great in a relationship? What great thing(s) do you bring to a relationship? Don't go to, "Well, this time, I don't want to be so jealous." That's not focusing on your magnificence so stop that!

You're only jealous because you didn't use the first three tools. Once you start receiving, know who you are at the soul level, and start listening, jealousy goes out the window. Because, if they trigger jealousy (which is usually lack of safety and trust), guess what, they are not-your-people.

Remember, what you're not good at in relationships is none of your business. Instead, by using the principles of the Self-Acceptance tool, you will start expanding what you are good at in love and turn up the wattage there.

How could it not equal more happiness or success? The same goes with your art. Or with your writing. Whatever it is that you are looking to create, this is the key to help you get there.

As the famous Judy Garland so eloquently stated, "Always be a first-rate version of yourself, instead of a second-rate version of someone else."

I've got to be my best Andrea Quinn. That's my job. I couldn't possibly be anyone else. Finding true empowerment in that only comes by using the tool of Self-Acceptance.

Don't dim your light.

I know when you were young, you were probably made to feel bad about being magnificent. Most of us were. How many times have we been told not to shine so bright or not to be such a "know-it-all" or lectured on how NOT to stand in our greatness because it might make other people feel uncomfortable in our presence.

Here's the thing, it isn't arrogant to know that you're magnificent. It's arrogant to continuously play small because Source, the Universe, God, Goddess, whomever or whatever you believe in, gave you those gifts in their omnipotent perfect wisdom before your birth. As Lady Gaga would say, "You were born this way." It is arrogant to think you know better and to think the gifts you have been given are "too small or not enough."

One of the thought leaders I admire is Marianne Williamson. She has been a pioneer in empowerment for women. In 1997, my life changed the minute I finished reading her first book, *A Return to Love*. That book had her famous quote called Our Deepest Fear.

"Our deepest fear is not that we are inadequate.
Our deepest fear is that we are powerful beyond measure.
It is our Light, not our Darkness, that most frightens us.

We ask ourselves, who am I to be brilliant, gorgeous, talented,
fabulous?
Actually, who are you not to be?
You are a child of God. Your playing small does not serve the
World.
There is nothing enlightening about shrinking
so that other people won't feel unsure around you.
We were born to make manifest the glory of God that is within
us.
It is not just in some of us; it is in everyone.
As we let our own Light shine,
we consciously give other people permission to do the same.
As we are liberated from our own fear,
our presence automatically liberates others."

How's that for Self-Acceptance? "As we let our own Light shine..."
How many times have you dimmed your light to fit in? I have done
this myself too many times to count. But this road to Self-
Acceptance eloquently laid out by Marianne Williamson is a game
changer.

Maybe right now you're doubting it. Maybe you're thinking
that everybody else is perfect, but you are messed up. No. You just
haven't practiced Self-Acceptance and taken an inventory of your
gifts because you're too busy trying to be someone else instead of
being your best you.

It isn't arrogant to know that you're magnificent.

Sometimes women in my workshops tell me, "Andrea, you make it seem like there's no one better to be than you."

I always tell them, "What choice do I have? I've got to rock this thing." If I don't have an empowering, self-accepting relationship with myself, how will I create a happy life? Seriously, I didn't get to be "Angelina" this time. I've got to do me, and I've got to do this life well. And the key to that comes from being in Self-Acceptance and asking myself, "Hey. What am I good at?" Why? Because what I'm not good at is none of my business.

It no longer bothers me that I don't cook. In fact, sometimes I say to myself, "Oh, I want to have a big dinner party." And instead of worrying about how I can't cook, I know I can turn to anybody else and say, "Here's what I want to do. I want to throw a dinner party, so guess what I'm good at..."

Number one
I'm good at bringing nice people together.

Number two
I'm good at wine.

Number three
I'm good at setting a table.

Number four
I'm good at knowing people who cook.

Sounds like a dinner party to me!

Do you see what happens when I shut down worrying about not being able to cook? I shut down being embarrassed and, instead, I embrace what I know I'm good at. Because I can do that, I'm going to write a cookbook and I don't cook. I have dinner parties and I don't cook. Not being able to cook doesn't stop me from the things I love.

What are you keeping yourself back from because you think you can't do something? I know it's a big question but, thinking about this initiates a conversation with yourself and gives you the opportunity to begin the success plan to accomplish your dreams.

Success Story #1

I remember one night, after teaching this tool, it became very clear for one woman who realized, "Oh. Wait a minute. I make fabulous jewelry, but I don't do websites." She had delayed opening her jewelry business online for years and only sold to friends because she was marred down with the daunting task of learning how to build a site and learn social media. She realized she had been stuck because she felt she had to learn it and do it or it wouldn't happen, so that is why she didn't move forward. Once she understood Self-Acceptance, she made that decision right then and there, "I'm really good at jewelry. Someone else will do the website." When, as she likes to say, she "was given permission

to do what she does well," it gave her the power to contact someone to do what they do well, which is a website.

She launched her online site only 30 days after the class and has been selling jewelry consistently ever since.

That same principle goes for all of you reading this too. Especially those of you thinking, "I've got to do this" or "I need to get a little better at that." Or, how about this one, "I'll get in a relationship, when I lose a little more weight."

Come on ladies, enough! You're magnificent already. Your job from now on is to be engaged in Self-Acceptance.

And I know this list of magnificence is hard for my overachievers. I know that if I were to say to you, "Okay. Give me a list of every place that you would like to change or improve," you'd have 10 things written instantly because you are so good at the improvement "to do" lists.

When you honor your gifts, it not only improves your life, but it also improves the life of every person who interacts with you. It brings to light where you contribute to the world and allows others to contribute with their gifts. Self-Acceptance is an act of generosity. (Did you ever think of that?)

None of your gifts and talents are small.

In my workshops, I like to tell the story of Mata Amritanandamayi Devi, also known as Amma.

Amma is a Hindu spiritual leader in India who is referred to as the "hugging saint" by her followers. If you don't know her, you should google her.

Amma exemplifies unconditional love and as you stand in front of her, she hugs you. She doesn't say a word to you; she just holds you.

People are healed in that moment. To date, she has held over 33 million people all over the world throughout the last 30 years. She is profound and when you are in the presence of that sweetness, you are healed forever.

Now what if, when Amma was a young girl in her twenties, she had said, "I don't know. I have no talents and I'm only good at one thing and it's hugging. It's just not enough. I have no real skills."

Instead, against her parent's wishes, she refused to get married and, because of her hugs, she has since made millions and millions of dollars for her foundation, which provides clean water for tens of millions of people, constructed tens of thousands of homes for those around the world who are homeless, provided free medical treatment and surgeries for people in need, and runs hundreds of orphanages.

She has said, "I don't see if it is a man or a woman in front of me. I don't see anyone different from my own self. A continuous stream of love flows from me to all of creation. This is my inborn nature. The duty of a doctor is to treat patients. In the same way, my duty is to console those who are suffering."

All of that from her hugs. Can you see now how everything you're good at is not small.

In breaking down that last story, we see that something as simple as hugging someone has created a "love and healing" movement all over the world. Think about the enormity of that. Think about how hard you are on yourself and how your gifts are never small, you just aren't looking at them through the lens of Self-Acceptance.

I met a woman who told me, "Andrea, I have no talents other than I can bake and I don't want to be a baker." I asked, "What do you do with the things you bake?" She told me she gives them to people she loves to make them happy.

Then I said "So, you take multiple ingredients, put them together to create something out of love that makes people feel good." She said, "Yes, I guess that's what I do." I replied, "Can you see that it isn't about baking? It's about the fact that you can creatively put things together with the intent to make people happy and from the Self-Acceptance of that, you can begin searching for your perfect job or career, and it doesn't have to be baking!"

Self-Acceptance will release you from the responsibility of being perfect and having to know it all.

Everything you have, every talent, every gift, you can be successful with or you can create happiness for the world, but you've got to stop trying to fix what is broken. Instead, figure out what's right with you, figure out where you rock, where you're already fabulous, and start a success plan with the expansion of your Self-Acceptance. How could you not achieve what you wish to accomplish?

Tools in Motion

1. List talents and gifts you have. List the first 10 things. If you have a hard time with this one, then ask a trusted person in your life. (Important note: Do NOT ask anyone whose approval you are seeking.)

2. Ask yourself where do you have talents or gifts that relate to what you want to accomplish? What are they? Identify them and start a success plan by looking at ways to expand them.

3. What are you keeping yourself back from because you think you can't do it? How can you apply your gifts to it and look to receive assistance from someone who is good at the things you are not?

Good to Know

1. Here's where I'm magnificent, and I can fully accept it.
2. Everything you're good at is a gift.

3. Lady Shame feels real, but it is just an illusion.

4. If you're going to be successful, you must acknowledge your gifts.

5. Don't dim your light.

6. It isn't arrogant to know that you're magnificent.

7. None of your gifts and talents are small.

Continuing the Conversation

To align deeper with this tool, join me for a video, which will shine a brighter light on Self-Acceptance.

http://www.thequinnessentials.com/self-acceptance/

or scan QR code

Section Two

Everything on the Outside

Chapter V
CONNECT

Everyone you need is right in front of you.

Congratulations! You've made it over halfway through the tools!

Hopefully, you've made sure to take the time to go through the Tools in Motion at the end of each chapter, reviewed the 'Good-to-Know's, and have been able to ask yourself some important questions. Trust that the questions you're asking yourself in these chapters will help you have both a deeper relationship with these tools and with yourself as time goes on.

As I mentioned in the beginning of this book, the first four tools are everything that you need to align with from the inside. Because you're working on them internally, the first four tools can sometimes feel almost alienating from the world. That's okay and don't worry if that's how it's showing up for you. I'm asking you to figure out what you want to align within yourself before you take it out into the world. To accomplish your dreams, it's important, as a woman, for you to have an empowered inner life as a foundation in order to have an empowered outer life. The next four tools will take you back out into the world.

In the following chapters, as you move from your inner world and begin doing some of the new exercises out in the world, you'll start to notice a change. And after the sixth tool, something truly magical happens. You'll find suddenly that you won't have to be thinking so much about the first four tools because they'll start showing up for you on their own!

To connect is to bring two things together. To establish a link between one another so that something greater is created. And what better way to illustrate Tool Number Five, Connect than by filling this chapter with examples of the magic that happens when women step out of their comfort zones and connect. These are stories from the lives of women who have used these tools and have shared their wonderful connection experiences with me and others. Hopefully, this is when things really start moving for you and you will begin to sink into that, *"Oh, this is something I can do right now!"* kind of feeling.

Connection is life.

You've got to Connect with people in this world if you're going to accomplish your dreams. No one does anything alone. No one. That is one of life's great secrets. We are all here for connection. (In fact, the only reason any of us are alive is because two people connected.)

Unfortunately, all too often, women don't connect because they're afraid of going outside of their comfort zone, telling themselves they think they already know who someone is, so why should they even try.

Seriously, ask yourself, how many times have you heard that loop play in your head about the people around you? When we've got our 'judgy' hats on, we say things to ourselves like, "Well, they're a nurse what do they know about real estate?... Or they do this, but I do that, so it would never work. Or I'm not into what they're into, so why bother..."

But moving forward, I want you to ask yourself this question, "How do you know that the one person you're waiting to meet in this lifetime to guide you to the next phase of your life isn't already someone in your orbit?" You don't know, do you? None of us know. We think we're protecting ourselves and saving our energy. Meanwhile, what we're actually doing is limiting ourselves and spending a lifetime struggling to accomplish our dreams because we have created a habit of not truly connecting with people. Think of how that energy could be used towards creating your accomplishments if you just made that one connection with the right person.

Now, I know you may be saying to yourself, "Wait a minute. I do connect with people!" And, if you're in that group, great! But now I want you to ask yourself, "Who exactly are you connecting with? Are you repeatedly connecting in your circle with the same people who you already know can't help you?" Just because you have an outgoing personality or always seem to be networking doesn't mean you are a good connector. I have had women for many years tell me at the beginning of this tool that they are so amazing at connecting with people but, by the end, have had their eyes opened to expanding their views of true connection and their minds and hearts unlocked in a new way.

Anything is possible through human connection.

As women, we have developed the art of summing up people before we really know them. We make sure they fit into a particular box before we connect with them while the truth is that the magic comes when we don't put anyone in a box. Connections come to us from an energetic alignment and the more we align from a non-judgmental place the higher energy we attract.

What I am talking about is connecting with those outside of your circle. Connect to those people! Talk to other human beings. How do you know that old lady next door with the three cats in the window isn't the grandmother of your future husband or wife? You don't. You just think you do.

This is what we do out in the world. Our fears make us so judgmental that we think we know, and we've already made up our mind. Instead, I want you to now be open to the possibility that even the person pouring your coffee in the morning could change the trajectory of your life.

—————————— $\mathcal{C}$ ——————————

As we all know 2009-2010 was a really tough time for a lot of people. Especially in Detroit. There was a young woman in one of my workshops in Los Angeles who is an actress but at the time, was working morning shifts at a coffee shop to support herself. Every morning she had a customer who would sit in the same corner with his computer and phone and work.

Everyone there could just feel the way he looked down on them with this huge attitude. He wouldn't even say hello to anyone other than the manager. He was so unpleasant that they would argue over who had to take his table. That's how bad he was. This went on for almost a year, until one day on her shift, magic happened. When she went to refill his coffee, she saw that had his hands over his face and was crying at his computer.

As she poured his coffee, she asked, "Are you okay?"

He brushed her off and said, "Yeah, I'll be fine. I'll be fine."

But she is Kindness and so she asked again, "Are you sure? Is there anything else I can get you?"

"No, no, no," he said. "You wouldn't understand (as if to say, 'you are just a waitress') and you wouldn't get this."

But before she could walk away, he was so distraught that he started talking and went on to say, "It's just the worst thing ever. I have a family business in Detroit. My great grandfather built it and it's been in the family for over a hundred years but we're about to lose everything. I've done everything I can to save it. I'm just devastated. I'm devastated for my family and for my parents."

She looked shocked and said, "Maybe my dad could help."

He was like, "What?"

She told him, "My dad's in the same business too, in Pennsylvania."

It so happens that her father was a billionaire in the same industry but when she moved to Los Angeles, he said that he wouldn't support her as an actor. He had told her that if she wanted to be an actor, she needed to get a job and take care of herself. Acting was so important to her that she said, "Okay" and started working to support her career.

The customer was stunned as she called her father on the spot. She put them on the phone together and they talked for a little bit about what was going on with his family's business. A few weeks later, her father flew out from Philadelphia to Detroit, gave them a convertible note so that the family could pay him back in four or five years, which they did by 2015.

That girl pouring his coffee saved him, his family business of 110 years and all its employees. Talk about the power of connection!

There are so many stories of women in my workshops who prove again and again that when we start connecting, looking at others with fresh and non-judgmental eyes, we can accomplish anything.

So instead of thinking, "you just pour my coffee" or "you're just washing my hair at the salon" or "you're just parking my car" or "you're just the UPS person in my building," open yourself up to what can happen when we look at this other human being with respect and "Connect."

Going to Starbucks is like a surprise party for me. I go in to order, there's a bunch of people there and it's awesome. My husband is the opposite. He says, "Okay, here's my order. Don't make any friends and don't bring anyone to the car to meet me." (Obviously we have different personalities.)

If I'm in line for a long enough period of time, I'm going to talk to somebody. I'm going to compliment a pair of shoes. I'm introducing myself, asking their name and starting a conversation. It's just the way it is. Sometimes I'll mess with my husband because I know he doesn't want me to bring people to the car to meet him, so I'll walk out talking to people. I can see him in the car saying to himself, "She's going to do it again. She's going to bring someone to the car." (I just love messing with him!)

Also, when I order our coffees, I personally acknowledge the barista. "Well, hey Tim. (Making sure I call him by his name from his badge.) I'd love to receive a cappuccino." (Notice the word receive) and just like magic I'm Connecting. I'm having a ball. They're thinking, this woman hasn't even had caffeine yet! Why am I so excited? Because what I know is that here's an opportunity for me to continue to practice connecting. Or maybe, there's a person in line I'm meant to connect with for someone else so that I can connect the two of them and they can accomplish something together. Who knows? The possibilities can be endless but not if you don't connect. Anything is possible through human connection! (Especially love.)

Good Girl syndrome is keeping you back.

For those who want to find love, somebody knows your next relationship or how to find them. It's a fact. You just don't know exactly how or who yet. So, the answer to that is to be open to people outside of your immediate circle and expand it through connection.

Another woman I have had the pleasure of knowing for many years wanted to get married and decided that the best way to meet her future husband was to Connect. She was so committed to it that she used to walk up to people at social events and say, "Excuse me, do you know my husband?" And they'd laugh and say, "We didn't know you were married." She'd reply with, "I'm not. Do you know him?" It was hilarious and she was also on the right path.

She had decided that she was done with the singles thing. And she was right, someone did know her husband. They introduced her to him and they are now married.

It's time to stop having Good Girl syndrome. You know that thing we do where we don't want to "bother" people. It's time to get over it! These stories are real. Just think, when you connect with someone, you aren't just helping yourself. By connecting with others, you're extending your resources to them as well. Good Girl syndrome is holding you back when it comes to meeting people. Women feel they have to have it all together in order to connect, but since you have been practicing Tools 1 through 4 by now, you can see that is a thing of the past – Good Girl begone!

Everyone you need to connect with is right in front of you, but if you don't see them because you have all of these 'to-do's or 'to-be's before connecting, then they will not manifest and contribute to your accomplishments. Have you ever heard the saying "the Universe is always working on your behalf"? I know it doesn't always feel like it, but the connections are there swirling around you even if you are working from home and living alone, all you have to do is open yourself to the practice of connecting.

Success Story #2

As you are aware, corporate layoffs are no joke. So many women have fallen victim to the downsizing of corporations and organizations and the numbers are staggering from 2019 to today. One woman who had attended my workshop right before she was unexpectedly laid off, said to me that connecting saved her! She was a Vice President at a large agency in Los Angeles and was laid off after 15 years when the agency merged with another one. She was single, helped her mother financially, and

had no net to catch herself. To say she was scared is an understatement.

Every day she had been home grieving, planning, applying for jobs and working LinkedIn, but to no avail. She only had so much time to get another job before her severance ran out and it seemed like time was going by too fast.

Because she was uncharacteristically home during the day, (obviously this story is before 2020) she began to see her mailman on a regular basis. She would wave and acknowledge him, but frankly she didn't know him at all. He had been her mailman for 10 years and she didn't even know his name!

One day she had a package delivered so he rang the bell to get her signature and they exchanged niceties. He told her he had noticed that she had been home for a while and was wondering if she was okay. She let him know she had been laid off and was trying to find employment. He knew she had something to do with the entertainment business (from the 10 years of delivering her mail) but had no idea what she did. She told him where she had worked and what she did there, and he said "That's a small world. My sister works at a different agency. I can connect you to see if there are any opportunities at her firm."

He told her to connect with his sister on LinkedIn and he would text her to accept and set up a coffee. And that's exactly what happened. Not only did she meet with his sister, but she also *interviewed for a position with her agency and in no time was employed again – All from connecting with her mailman!*

We're on this earth to connect with one another.

The previous story is a perfect example of people crossing our path every day and yet we do not know them or haven't properly connected with them. There are all types of excuses we come up with... "I'm too busy," "I've never talked with them before" and "I'm sure we have nothing in common" are just a few of the daily excuses we use not to properly connect. In fact, I don't even think we are aware of how often we use them. With our phones in our hands, we are now such a distracted society that we do not even look up to greet each other. I now make an effort to leave my phone in the car so that I can authentically connect with other people. We could be missing out on the connections to people who can help us with our accomplishments even if they're right in front of us. Since teaching and implementing the tools for myself, I've looked at the people who pour my coffee or deliver my mail so differently. I have heard the many "Connect" stories over the years and they have profoundly changed my life as well. The truth is in connecting with others we don't know who they are or what they think or who they know. And you also don't know how you can help them.

When women connect, they start helping each other and they change each other's lives. That's the beauty of it. This is why we are alive. We are on this Earth to connect with one another. It's not only important, but also essential.

Connection is community.

Later on, in this chapter's Tools in Motion, I'm going to invite you to Connect outside of your circle of safety. And I'd like to invite you to practice connecting even if you think you're really, really bad at it or if you're really, really shy. Trust me, I get it. I really do. One of the things about me that is usually hard for my clients to believe is that I'm actually much more of a homebody even though my business is, by nature, very social. So, I truly understand how hard this can be for some people. But it's a tool I work on because I also know that the beauty of connecting will change my life in the process.

I want you to focus on moving away from the fears that are holding you back from the change you want in your life. Start to see this as your chance to connect with that one person you have been wanting to connect with. Even though you may think you have every reason not to. Maybe you don't think you're good enough or experienced enough. Or maybe you think you don't want to bother them. Remind yourself that is fear talking. Remember this is where you must get out of your head and be open to receiving that connection, which will be an important step towards actualizing your accomplishments.

So, commit to taking one step at a time, no matter how small you think it is. You know that person that you just thought of? That's the one! Take that one step outside of your immediate circle and Connect with them. It can even be as simple as a LinkedIn invitation to start.

Connection is community. Connection is what we're missing. If 2020 has taught us anything, it is how important human beings and our connections to each other are. Connecting is more important than ever since we have experienced first-hand as a global community what separation actually looks and feels like.

Success Story #3

Another woman in one of my workshops moved from London and took a job as a teacher at one of the prestigious design schools in Los Angeles. In addition to teaching, she also created her own beautiful, incredible line of toys for big retail stores and designed stationery and paper products.

When she listed her Accomplishments, she had told us, "One of the things I want to do is to design private label stationary and wrapping paper for a very large retail brand here in the U.S."

As a self-proclaimed introvert, she had lived in one of those cute bungalow communities in Venice, California for six years but had never socialized with anybody. Not a single neighbor.

Instead, she would just come home with her little dog, shut her shades, and do her thing. So... I asked her to Connect.

She told us she had come home one night and, while usually hearing her neighbors and immediately looking down in order to avoid eye contact, this evening she knew to look up in order to fulfill her "homework" from the class and Connect.

She laughed as she told us the story, "So, I looked over and there was a gentleman about three doors down. He looked into my eyes, I looked into his eyes, and then I panicked. I didn't know what to do. So, you know how Barbie has that arm that's stuck at an awkward angle... I gave him the Barbie arm." She is so proper that we could visualize it completely and were on the floor laughing with her.

She knew that her neighbor was just as shocked as she was because he'd never connected with her before. So, he kind of waved, went inside, and shut the door behind him. Again, being an introvert, she said, "Well, I did my exercise for the workshop, done with that." The funny thing is, from that moment on, when he would be out walking with his wife, they would wave at her, and she would wave back. She was so proud of herself, "I'm waving at my neighbors!"

One Sunday she heard a knock at her door. She looked and saw that it was the couple who she had waved to down the street. She was taken aback but opened the door with a polite "Hello."

"Hi, we haven't properly introduced ourselves. I'm Paul."

"And I'm Susan. How long have you lived here?"

"Oh, almost six years now," she answered.

"Wow, we've been here about three years. We hadn't seen you before, so we wanted to drop off these flyers for our annual neighborhood barbecue. We have the barbecue so that everyone can get to know each other in the community, see their children, dogs, etc. It's very similar to a neighborhood watch group so we can take care of each other."

"Oh, lovely." (This was really one of her biggest fears hence not socializing with her neighbors in the first place and she instantly became annoyed with them and me.)

They continued, "Well, it's next Saturday. And everybody brings something. If you can make it, we could always use a salad. We take care of the meats but need a lot of side dishes."

She told them she might have plans, thanked them for dropping off the flyers and shut the door. She didn't even want to meet one neighbor let alone all of them but... Connect... Connect... Connect... So, she apprehensively changed her mind and decided she was going to show up, bring a salad, say hello, and grab some wine in a plastic cup. She told herself she would stay for maybe 15 minutes tops.

Saturday came and she headed over to the community barbecue with her salad. As Susan, the wife of the couple started talking to her, they began to connect. "What do you do?" Susan asked. "I am a creative. I teach; I design my own line of toys and

I also design stationery and paper products." Susan responded with an animated, "Oh, that's fantastic!"

Just then Paul, Susan's husband came over from manning the grill.

Susan said, "Paul, we've got to have her over some time. She's a designer and a teacher."

Paul says, "Really? That's great."

*And then Susan turned back to her and said, "My husband commutes back and forth from the East Coast and he is the president of the private label division of this large retail chain." Can you guess what retail brand that was? Yes, it was the exact retail stores she had wanted to design for.... **BOOM!!!!***

True story. He was living three doors down from her FOR THE LAST THREE YEARS. Again, I have hundreds and hundreds of these stories that women have shared with me over the years.

Think about it... Who's living three doors down from you that you don't know? Why are your walls up? Who are you not seeing? Who have you already summed up? Who doesn't know you yet because of this self-imposed block in your ability to connect with other human beings? This is what prevents us from getting to where we need to go.

Connection takes your life to the next level.

I want to share one last *Success Story* with you that so perfectly illustrates how the people who can help you accomplish your dreams are right there in front of you; and probably have been there the whole time waiting for you to take your connection to the next level. Taking something to the next level is nothing more than an empowered expansion and I guarantee that this tool will do this in every area of your life. The greater your circle of people the greater the opportunities. The breadth and width of your ability to connect determines the amount of energy that comes towards you as you are accomplishing your dreams.

Success Story #4

Yet another woman in a workshop started turning green on the night we discussed Connect. I mean all different shades of green. When I asked her if she was okay, she said, "I think I'm going to be sick."

"Why?"

"I'm an editor," she explained. "I sit in a room by myself all day."

"What do you want to accomplish," I asked.

"Well, I created a reality TV show and I want to accomplish pitching and selling my show."

She had developed a show for women and there were only about three production companies that could even do her show because of the size of the production. It was a big and amazing idea. It was, in fact, so fantastic that I watched the trailer over and over just so that I could feel the hairs stand up on my body. She had been working on this project for about six years to get it to where it was and everybody who had seen it knew how special it was.

So, I asked, "Well, do you think you're going to meet these people in an editing bay?"

"No."

"Then you have to Connect."

"Oh, I hate connecting," she says.

"I get it. But you have to Connect, or nothing will happen." A mom of two, she was an editor at a major studio in Hollywood with late hours and so she never finished work early enough to watch her son's little league baseball games. Her son had played on this same team with these same boys for 5 years. On the rare nights she was able to catch a game, she would just stand by the car, and watch from afar so she didn't have to sit and talk to the parents of the other boys. Her son would wave at her from the field, and she would wave back from her car. Sometimes she would offer up a courtesy smile at people, but she never connected with anyone beyond that.

One night she got out of work in time to make it to his game...

Earlier that week, we had finished our workshop on Connect. So, when we met up for the next Tool, she said, "Andrea, I heard your voice in my head to go talk to people."

So, this time, with my voice in her head, she walked over to the bleachers instead of standing by her car alone. She quietly slid onto the seats and looked around hoping no one had noticed. But you know there's always that one parent who is the mayor of the group? For this crew, the mayor was a guy named Bob and he was the loudest parent for sure. And Bob knew EVERYONE.

Bob looked over at her and said, "Well, hey, there."
(Because she had never connected with anybody before, no one even knew her name.)

Bob continued, "We never see you here. How's it going?"
"Good, I got off a little early today."
Bob asked, "Oh really, what do you do?"
"I work as an Editor."
"Oh, really cool. That's great."

And then she remembered "connection means taking it to the next level."

She took a deep breath, cursed me in her mind, and said, "But I'm working on producing my own reality show."
Bob replied, "Oh really? What's it about?"

She told him about her show and without skipping a beat, Bob said, "Oh, that's so interesting. I'm in reality television. I own a production company. You might want to come in and talk to us."

It turned out that Bob owned one of the three larger reality production companies I had mentioned earlier! Bob, right there, in the same stands, watching the same games with her for five years. He had been in her orbit for 5 years! You just can't make this stuff up!!!

Everyone you need is right in front of you. Always. Everywhere you go, in every part of your life, they are there. You just think they're not because maybe you think they're too old. Or they're too young. They're too this; they're too that. And you tell yourself to forget it. Whatever that is for you, you need to stop making those assumptions. Stop summing things up in your head and telling yourself that you're sure they don't know. Because as you've seen in the Success Stories, you don't know.

Story after story like these happen. When you start connecting, the stories you're going to have are going to be amazing too. You'll say, "I never knew... I never knew she was my neighbor... I said hello to him for 10 years and I never knew."

As you take this out into the world, talk to someone you wouldn't normally talk to. Even if it's someone you work with. Maybe it's the security guard in your office building or your mail person.

Connect.

Connect.

Connect.

Find out anything about them or where they're from. Don't just wave at them and go about your day. That's not Connection. Take it to whatever that next level is for you.

And if you're one of those people who talks to everyone already, then find the one person you really want to talk to that you've been avoiding. Connect with that person online if that's an easier start for you. It can be that simple. The important thing is that you are stepping into a connection right now. Let it be with someone you really want to connect with that takes you out of your comfort zone. Those are especially exciting because of all the wonderful surprises that can come from connecting with someone in a way you hadn't before.

When you step outside of your group, outside of any fear you may be holding onto and expand your entire world, that's when magic happens!

Tools in Motion

1. Connect with someone you would normally not say hello to. Make an effort to speak to them even if you simply wish them a good day. Start with small steps if connecting is hard for you.

2. Go into a store or coffee shop and leave your phone in the car. (I know your list is on your phone, but you can write it out on

paper to interrupt your pattern of always looking at the phone. And if you have an app to pay for it then leave it in your handbag or backpack, ringer off and don't pick up the phone until you are at check out. You will feel uncomfortable in the beginning, but each time it will get easier and easier.)

3. Take a look at your Accomplishment list and write next to it the top person you must connect with for each accomplishment. Then, reach out! Dive in! The water's great!

4. Go deeper in a relationship with someone you are already speaking with in your life. Practice connecting at a broader level on a regular basis and keep a journal on the expansion of your life and circle. (There will be obvious markers in this journal due to you connecting in a deeper way.)

Good To Know

1. Connection is life.
2. Anything is possible through human connection.
3. Good Girl syndrome is keeping you back.
4. We are on this earth to connect with one another.
5. Connection is community.
6. Connection takes your life to the next level.

Continuing the Conversation

To continue with this tool, please join me for a video, which will assist you in expanding your ability to connect.

http://www.thequinnessentials.com/connect/

or scan QR code

Chapter VI

ASK

**Because you don't know what you don't know,
ask everyone you know.**

Hands up as we reach the top of the roller coaster with Tool Number Six, **ASK**! This Tool is probably the one that is the most powerful for me personally and has the greatest impact for the World. (Since 2009 while teaching this tool, I am always brought to tears due to the enormity of this concept.)

On the road to accomplishing your dreams, you must Ask. You will need to have the courage of a warrior to ask for what you want. I think archetypically of the great Joan of Arc because she so perfectly embodies the courage that I know it takes to step out of our comfort zones to Ask.

Asking is so important it's even mentioned in the Bible, "...Ask, and ye shall receive, that your joy may be made full." (John 16:24) It doesn't say, "Ask and I'll think about it, and then after a few karmic tests, I'll get back to you." No. It says, "Ask and ye shall receive." And, if you study Abraham-Hicks, their big book, *Ask and It Is Given* is even named after that verse. Asking is that necessary.

Asking is also another form of Receiving. And we receive so that we can, what? Create.

I know, typically, women don't want to ask because it makes us very uncomfortable. I hear it all the time. We don't want to put anyone out. We don't want to offend anyone. We don't want to make anything hard on them in any way. We are so uncomfortable we feel we need to make sure we are ready and worthy before we can ask. So, out of our graciousness and our fabulous natures, we will not bother you with an Ask. #GoodGirlSyndrome.

If you're one of the many women who find it really hard to ask for themselves and often use the excuses I just listed, great, because in this chapter, I am going to cure you of what I call "ask-itis"!

Ask-itis is a term I use for the self-imposed sick feeling we have when we put ourselves out there to ask for what we want to receive. It creates so many thoughts and emotions that it holds most of us back.

First, I'm going to guess that you don't have a problem asking for anyone else. That you may even find it easy to ask others things like, "Hey, could you hire this person?" Or "Could you fund this for those people who are less fortunate?" And especially "Could you do this for this group?" But what do you do when it's time to ask for yourself? Do you hold back and lock it down? Do you come down with a case of "Ask-itis"? If so, there is a cure!

Our lives can never manifest if we don't ask. You cannot have a successful life as an isolationist. It's just not going to work. And, trust me, I get it. I know what it's like to not want to ask. I was an expert at not asking until 2009 when at a Peace Conference in Canada, the Dalai Lama said these words, "The world will be saved by the western woman."

All of my excuses around not asking fell apart because of that one statement. If you've heard it before, great. If you haven't heard it before, I want you to let it sink in for a moment...

This world will be saved by the Woman.

The expanded truth of the Dalai Lama's statement is, "the world will be saved by Women, empowered women all over the world." Who do you think you are? Yes, that statement applies to you! If you are reading this book, chances are you are a privileged woman in some way or another. (There are so many less fortunate than us and sometimes we lose perspective.) You may walk around like you're not worthy of anyone giving you anything but now is the moment to put that to a full stop.

Here's one of the biggest secrets to get you there... You must understand that it isn't only about asking for what you currently want to receive. Asking must be about the endgame. And endgame is synonymous with your legacy or what you want to do for this world. It's about knowing that every single Ask (big and small) is about the endgame. When I heard the proclamation from the

Dalai Lama, I knew I no longer had any other options. I have got to bring this home and I can no longer hold back out of fear. There is a world to save, and it is depending on all of us. Dust off your capes, ladies!!!

The only reason you're afraid to ask for things for you is because you're making it about **you**. Your ego is speaking and taking charge. You're thinking, "Well, I want them to give me this opportunity, but I don't want to bother them." Really?!? Yes, you do. You just need to know why you're doing it and to see how much bigger than you it is.

I'll let you in on a little secret. Personally, I have an endgame to what I do. I have an enormous need to empower women so that I can knock out what is one of the world's biggest killers - Stress. Because, when a woman is stressed out, she makes some of the biggest mistakes of her life. When we are mentally stressed, we make bad decisions. When we're emotionally stressed, we make bad decisions. When we're spiritually stressed, we make bad decisions. Bad decisions are the road to more unhappiness and more stress. We've heard it over and over; for both men and women. Stress is the number one killer. I want to create centers to assist people around the world in receiving support in dealing with stress so they can make empowered decisions for their lives. Yes, that's my endgame!

The golden rule is the one with the gold makes the rules.

We've become so afraid to ask – because of what they'll think of us or how they'll judge us – that we are keeping our greatness from the world. Children are starving. There are people without water, without beds, without food. This planet is dying. **And you're afraid to ask because of what "they" will think of you?** What must you think of yourself for not recognizing the value you can bring to the world? Or we judge our "Ask" as not big enough. If it's just because you're intimidated by those who make the money, then know that your asking is to make the money too so you can fund your endgame.

The golden rule is the one with the gold makes the rules. We tell ourselves that we're helpless at times because we don't have the money to change or to even lobby for the changes we want. Imagine the possibilities that open when you just start asking and decide that you will make the gold so that you can change those rules that need to be changed.

If you're an actress and you think, "Well, I want them to put me in their movie." Great. That Ask could get you the break you need so that you become famous. And when you become famous, you have a platform to speak to a larger audience about your endgame. (By the way, you do not need to be famous to get on a platform and start talking about your endgame, it's just an example of how we think something could be about us when, really, it's about the world.) Every job, every connection, every accomplishment is the road to healing this world **IF** you will play a bigger game!

A lot of women have *"When-syndrome,"* which is a side effect of Ask-itis. *When-syndrome* is what happens when we project allowing ourselves to achieve success onto the future. We must earn the right through accomplishing tasks before we can allow ourselves to receive. "When I get this, I'll do that." "When they give me my stuff, I'll help you." The world cannot be changed or healed while you suffer from *when-syndrome.* The time is NOW! Going back to Chapter One, ask yourself "What first step could I receive towards my accomplishment and who should I ask?" Great question, right?

I have women who say to me they don't want their successful friends or community to think that they want anything. Yes, you do! You want to receive by asking so you can heal this world! This is not a small thing! Can you imagine how quickly the world could change if all women just did this for one day? It gives me goosebumps.

You want your dreams to come true so you can help others. Famous or not, wealthy or not, if they really are your friends, they're going to want to help you. And if they're no longer your friends because you asked, then what? Then they are not-your-people – or your true friend.

Stop worrying about what people will think of you for asking. Instead, take that precious energy and think about who you can help now as well as down the road when you've achieved all that you're looking to accomplish. They need you. Stop worrying about it and just do it.

Success Story #1

There was a woman who was gifted The Quinn Essentials Workshop by her friends because she had gone through a tough time, and they thought it would help her. She lost her hair salon business, her home, her love relationship, which included his children from a previous partnership, and her self-worth. It was a very dark time for her and as she listened to me speak on the Ask tool, she began to see how the solutions to give her some peace and support were right in front of her, but she was too afraid to ask. She confessed to me that she was in judgment about the situation "she had gotten herself into" and her ego was convincing her she had to jump through hoops to prove her worth in order to ask for help. She was becoming physically ill from all the stress and could not see any way out.

Her best friend who grew up with her and lived on her street is a wonderful man. When he chose to come out, she stood by him as they grew up and they navigated many years of life together. They were now in their 40s and still very close.

He was aware of her dark time and was there for her, but because she was acting as if she had the situation under control, he was unaware of the depth of the stress she was enduring. He was VERY successful and had always taken her on trips and given her beautiful gifts. His generosity was something she both loved and felt guilty about receiving because she could not reciprocate. She knew after the workshop that he was right there and her shame prevented her from Asking. She needed to receive the money to get out of debt, pay off her business partner who was extorting her and start her life again. After sitting up all night, finally honestly reflecting on her situation, she came to peace with asking. She also asked herself, "How can I heal this world?"

She knew how important stories are to the healing of people and even though she had made her living as a hairdresser, she was always looking to get into production by buying rights to stories that would heal people from their pain. Her endgame is telling the stories we need to hear about people overcoming what we are going through and give people the permission to not give up.

The next morning, she called him and asked him for a loan. She let him know she would pay him back as soon as she could, that she was not doing okay, and really needed to receive help. He was shocked and saddened to hear what she had truly been going through and was happy to help. She asked for $75,000 and *he gave her $200,000. He told her it was not a loan but a gift. He loved and believed in her just like she believed in him. She was so overwhelmed, to say the least. A short time later, I was so happy to receive two photos from her; one was the deposit slip to the bank and the other was her on her way with him to Europe in first class because he thought she needed a vacation after all this stress. Today she is still a very successful hairdresser, helps women financially and has a script purchased at a major studio with production deals being worked out now.*

The story above shows how asking and receiving can work together in harmony. You can see how "everyone she needed was already right in front of her." It is amazing to me how many women tell me their ego disguising itself as fear and judgment is the real enemy of asking. Once they face the ego head on, they can see that asking is imperative to moving forward. Another thing the above woman shared with me was how "asking" her friend wasn't even on the table in the beginning because she was "never going to cross that line." What she discovered once she did was how glad he was to help, how much more support she had offered him through life than she realized and how much she was loved. Don't we all want that?

'No' doesn't mean I'm not going to do it.
'No' just means I'm not going to do it with you.

That's the truth. In life, you have to trust those 'No's. "No, I'm sorry I can't help you," doesn't mean your idea is bad. It just means that's not your door. And remember, just because they say 'No,' it doesn't mean that they don't care.

I had a woman who wanted me to mentor her as a coach. I didn't have the time and so I said to her, "I adore you. I'm so glad you're going to be a coach, but I would be doing you a disservice if I took you on right now. It would be too much stress for me with my current schedule and therefore I couldn't give you the attention that you need. But please keep me posted on how you're doing. I believe in you as a coach; I just don't have the time."

You see, I wanted to help her, but in all fairness to both of us, it wouldn't have been right to mentor her at that time.

We've all had those things that we wanted so badly but we don't get. Then suddenly, years later we say, "Thank God, I didn't get that." There are even relationships where we beg, "Dear God, please let him or her love me. Please." Then time goes by, we run into them with their new person, and when we walk away, we say to ourselves, "Wow. Thank God, I didn't end up with them! Dodged that bullet."

Just remember that "Rejection is Protection" and if you get a 'No,' trust the Universe that it means your 'Yes' just hasn't arrived yet. Don't waste time worrying about it. A very important point to asking is that you do not attach yourself to the result. If you are asking, you didn't have whatever it was in the first place, so not getting it doesn't change anything but your direction. (You might want to review that sentence again.)

I love the example of Dr. Seuss. Dr. Seuss had his first kid's book rejected by 27 publishers until one afternoon as he was walking home, work in hand after the 27th rejection, he ran into an old college friend who asked him what he was carrying. His friend just happened to have been made an editor of children's books that morning, invited him up to his office, and he bought the book on behalf of the publisher that day. Dr. Seuss had found his people, his publisher, and the rest is history. He believed in what he was doing and later used his success to form the Dr. Seuss Foundation whose **mission is to expand literacy**. (Aka his endgame.)

This is what I'm talking about ladies. What is your endgame going to be?

One of the most upsetting things to me is when powerful women don't take their place at the proverbial table of success. They're afraid of their history, they're afraid of every perceived failure in their past. They are stuck in the internal dialogue of, "What if they don't like me anymore?" "What if it's a stupid idea?" "What if I don't have the credentials?" "What if I lose their money?"

Do it anyway!

What if Dr. Seuss had given up after the 12th rejection? Or even the 20th? And know that your idea as it is today may even morph into a different idea in five years becoming bigger and greater than you even thought possible. Asking will help you get there. Remember, you don't know what you don't know, so you might as well ask everyone you know.

Success Story #2

There was a woman in this community who is a television director and I asked her whose career she wanted to emulate. She said this particular male director who is beloved and has created so many of our favorite film and television shows with multiple nominations. She loved his work, public image, and brand.

She was in my workshop and a private client with me at that time. So, when she came in for her one-on-one session, I said, "You want to emulate his career? Call him."

She said, "What?"

I said, "Well, you're both members of the Director's Guild of America (DGA), call him and see if he'll have a mentor cup of coffee with you."

"I can't do that," she stammered.

"Sure, you can. We just started our session; we've got an hour. Let's do this. You're going to pick up the phone and you're going to call the DGA right now, you're going to get the phone

number to his office and you're going to see if he'll have a mentor cup of coffee. We've got nothing to lose."

She may have been glaring at me, but she made the call and because she is a DGA member, she received the number for his office. I was so excited for her. I said, "I'm going to go make tea." And I got up thinking there was a good chance she was going to leave while I was getting the tea.

When his office answered she said, "Hi, this is so-and-so, I'm with the Director's Guild, and I was wondering if Mr. Director (always keeping everyone anonymous) would ever be open for a mentor cup of coffee with a female director?"

"Hold please."

She was still holding when I came back but as I sat down, suddenly his office got back on the phone and said, "How would next Friday be at one o'clock?"

She was stunned it was that easy. She did the best she could to stay calm and take down all the information she needed for their meeting.

She hung up and I looked at her and said, "Now your work begins. You have this man, a mentor, for an hour. Do you know how much his time is worth? Please don't go down the list of all the movies you love that he's done and waste it. You have the person whose career you want. Ask intelligent questions, spend the rest of this week working on your questions, and then run them by me."

She met with him, sat in his office and had her cup of coffee with him. He talked to her and loved it. He mentioned that he was impressed that she wanted a mentor cup of coffee, and he was honored. At the end, he looked at her and said, "Hey, I had such a great time. You are such a nice lady. How about we do this mentor thing once a month for the rest of the year?"

And they did.

Let me be clear, this was not some hot 20-year-old writer who he found attractive and was preying on. This was a woman in her late 50s, who had beaten cancer three times. It was clear from the scars on her face that she had been through hell and back. The person whose career she wanted to emulate the most, had looked in her eyes and said, "I like you. You're a great lady."

They met for a cup of coffee every month and it changed the trajectory of her career and of her life.

This story shows that even if someone is super successful by the world's standards, they are human and human beings want to help other human beings.

I hope this tool is helping you change the lens on how you see asking. Who's currently doing what you want to do in your life and who is doing it successfully? Get a mentor meeting with someone you admire, receive the information from them that you need to take your accomplishments to the next level and do it your way. Ask so you can step fully into your greatness and save women from sex trafficking, help with the world's water shortage, whatever the change is that you would like to see in this world.

Ask for everything! If you don't get what you want, instead of thinking there is something inherently wrong with your idea, think of your Asks as being in the infancy stage. Know that there is absolutely nothing wrong with your ideas; you're just learning how to fine tune them. So go Ask everyone you know and let your ideas grow and form into the questions that they are meant to be to get the most support. Whatever it takes, give yourself permission.

Love is worth asking to receive.

A lot of this chapter has been about asking for money, opportunities or help in business. But what about love? If finding love is one of your accomplishments, you might be asking yourself, "How does that save the world?" Love is the only true thing that can change the world. Everything is about love when you break it down. Everything.

When you participate in a loving relationship you have the privilege in becoming a part of an extended group of people where you can make a contribution to their lives. There are so many ways to heal the world when love is the priority. Having a child with your mate who will change the world. Supporting children from a broken home with the engagement of a stepparent. Joining a new group of friends who start volunteering together for like-minded causes. Helping your partner with their elderly family and bringing love to them. The possibilities are endless and important because for every person loved, the resonance of the world goes up and healing can happen for the planet. I was fortunate to be very close to my mother-in-law and called her every day to make her feel loved, just as my husband gave so much of his energy to help my father even in his last days. Since love truly is the answer, can you see how important people coming together in love is to save this world? (Again, thank you Dalai Lama.)

We all have an endgame, what's yours?

Now we're going to use our imagination. Let's imagine that you have received everything you ever wanted, that whatever your accomplishment is, you've accomplished it. You've got all these resources, your family is taken care of, you've got everything aligned, and now it's your time to step up. So now where will you give your resources to save this world? We all have an endgame, so what's yours?

Write it down right here:

This is who you're asking for. You're not asking for you. You want the opportunity to take the next step in your life, the next step in your career, the next step of whatever it is so that you can get to that place where you can help others. That's why we're all here. And remember, the only reason you would feel awkward about asking anyone for anything is because you have yourself and your ego in front of it and you're making it about you.

The people on this above list are waiting for you, ladies. Ask yourself, are you going to stay afraid to ask or are you going to step into how important an impact you can make in this world? You are the Western Woman. As I shared with you earlier, I was fine until the Dalai Lama dropped that gem. Now I've got to do something about it. I'm living every day of my life focusing on that endgame.

You've got to ask and stop worrying about what they think of you. Understand your value. Don't worry about asking your friends. Trust that the Universe probably put them in your friendship circle for a reason. Remember, if the people that you ask to help you say they don't want to be your friend anymore because you asked, then now you know that they weren't really your friend to begin with. If they're your people, you've got nothing to worry about. If they're not-your-people, congratulations, you just practiced asking.

Ask until you're tired. Ask everyone you know.

Those people who are doing what you want to do? Get a mentor meeting. Ask to receive information from them. If you get nervous, that's okay, take a breath and remember why you're doing it. Write down your questions exactly as I had my client do before her own mentor meeting. Make sure you're prepared and know why you deserve to receive the meeting with them as well.

What are you here to do? Whatever that is, I want you to go out there and be the light that encourages people through your example.

Unfortunately, women tend to stop at a 'No.' When someone says, "No, I can't help you," it can shatter us. From now on, I want you to take on a "not my door" attitude when you get a No. Instead, keep looking for your 'Yesses' and hold onto your hat. I know, sometimes the 'Yesses' can scare the hell out of you. I get that. They just do. When that happens, return to your Why – the reason you have for why you're doing it and who you're saving in this world.

When you have that in mind, my question to you is why wouldn't you ask? You have so many things that matter. And so many people waiting for you to achieve greatness. They are waiting.

This truly is another power tool. When I ask something of someone, I'm asking in a way where they become a step in the process of it happening. If they say 'Yes' to me, I know it gets me to my next step. And when I take the step, I trust that it will take me to the step after, and so on and so on. When you ask from that power place, you're also raising the vibration of your Ask. And, trust me, the bigger you play vibrationally, the bigger the opportunities will be that come to you.

When you Ask, it may be for you but it's not about you.

Everything you are asking for is important not only to you but for the greater good. You cannot think about yourself alone or we won't be able to fix this world. When you approach it from that place, you begin to honor and empower yourself. There's no wrong way for you to ask anything from anyone. When you begin to play a bigger game in this world, it will manifest as a bigger life that you will lead. When you Ask for something, it is for you but it's not about you since it's all a road to your endgame. We don't have to wait until we are successful to begin this journey with greatness, we just have to Ask to receive the first step.

Wouldn't you prefer to be able to look yourself in the mirror having asked and not received what you wanted rather than looking in the mirror knowing that you had never asked out of fear?

I told you that "ask-itis" would be a thing of the past! You're cured! Anything you ask for isn't about you, it's about all the people waiting for you to help fulfill the Dalai Lama's prophecy. Let's go Ladies!!! Start asking! Receive your accomplishments! Save the World!

Tools in Motion

1. When looking at your accomplishment list, what are your asks? Who are you asking? When are you asking? Why are you asking? 2. What is the biggest Ask you are putting off and why? I want you to know you CAN ask! (Some women say no one has ever given them permission to ask, I just did. Go for it!)

3. Know what your endgame is. Who are you helping? Dig a little deeper into what you listed in this chapter. Write it down and start to do a little research around whatever it may be and how you can begin to move toward that endgame now even if you donate $10 a month to that cause, it begins the momentum.

4. What would change in your life if you asked? Where could you receive more support towards your accomplishments?

5. Practice asking. If you are good at it, go big! If it is hard for you, start small but ask for something every day, watch your confidence grow. If something doesn't come easy to us, we have to practice. Keep a list of your asks as you move forward with your accomplishments; it will chart your course.

6. Ask yourself, what 'No's have you received in your life that may have actually led to your successes.

Good To Know
1. This world will be saved by the Woman.

2. The golden rule is the one with the gold makes the rules.

3. 'No' doesn't mean I'm not going to do it. 'No' just means I'm not going to do it with you.

4. Love is worth asking to receive.

5. We all have an endgame, what's yours?

6. When you Ask, it may be for you but it's not about you.

Continuing the Conversation

For continued clarity of this tool, please join me for a video, which will make asking a part of your everyday life.

http://www.thequinnessentials.com/ask/

or scan QR code

Chapter VII

VISUALIZE

If you can't see it, you can't be it.

All right! So now that we've gone through Tools One through Six together, we're going to move right into Tool Number Seven, **Visualize!**

Visualize is defined as "to form a mental image – imagine." You already know how to do this since we do it all day long by default. But the magic to visualizing is to actually create the image you want to see or create the outcome to something before it happens.

You may already be familiar with the process of visualizing. If not, don't worry. I am going to teach you how to visualize. Even if you already practice visualizing, we are going to take it to the next level.

You may be wondering "if visualization is something that you think about, why am I including it as one of the tools that we do on the outside?" Great question and get ready for a powerful answer with access to this amazing process.

Here's the deal; If you can't see it, you can't be it. The bottom line is you must be able to see the life you want to live before you create it. In this chapter, we will start by creating the actual visualizations, then we will learn how to bring it to your outer world.

There are a lot of great books that discuss the importance of visualization such as, *THINK AND GROW RICH* by Napoleon Hill written in 1937 as well as the collective works of Florence Scovel Shinn who wrote *THE GAME OF LIFE AND HOW TO PLAY IT* in 1925.

But, with *CREATIVE VISUALIZATION*, Shakti Gawain hit the pulse of a new generation. In her book, she created a fresh way of bringing these concepts to the modern era, speaking to something that people were ready to hear once again. Since its first publication in the 1970s until today, this book has been a bestseller. Gawain was such an incredible guru and powerful educator; she was also one of the premier teachers and mentors to some of the great Thought Leaders of our time, Louise Hay, Deepak Chopra, Wayne Dyer and Ram Dass to name a few.

One of the most significant things with The Quinn Essentials Visualize tool is how my process is in alignment with Shakti's work. I am honored to say that she was familiar with my Quinn Essential Tools, and I was told she had given me her acknowledgment before she passed away in 2018. I greatly admired her and one of my favorite things that I own is my parents' yellowed first edition copy of *Creative Visualization* from the '70s.

Through her work, she teaches the reader how to create a visualization in their mind in such a way that it feels as if you are actually living and experiencing what you're seeing for yourself. Maybe you've experienced moments like this before. Moments where you were imagining something and suddenly your heart started racing. Like, in an "Oh, my God! It's as if I'm there!" sort of way. This is the magic of what happens when your physical body suddenly knows no difference between now and the future you are looking to create!

The first part of this tool is a combination of Creative Visualization's original process and my own. As we go along, you will see how I have "Quinn'ed it up."

There is no wrong way to visualize.

As we take a look at visualization and dive a bit deeper into The Quinn Essentials method, I want to free you from the fear of getting stuck on the "how" of visualization. Everybody does it differently so there is no wrong way of doing it. You don't even have to mentally see an image in your mind in order to make it "work." Some women can close their eyes and imagine, for example, a kitten running through a field. In their mind's eye, they can actually see a field with an actual kitten running in it. Whereas, some people can't see it, but they can feel it, understand it and know exactly what it is just the same. Neither way is better or worse. They are just simply different ways to access one of the major components in helping you reach your accomplishments.

I personally recommend visualizing what you want either before you go to bed at night or when you wake up first thing in the morning. I have found those are the times where we can do it from a very clear space; before the events of the day have clouded our mind or after we've been able to leave them all behind us for the night.

I will now share with you three key elements to visualizing. First, I'll use Gawain's language, and then I'll give you my own Quinn Essentials language. You'll see how related they are and how she inspired me as she has done millions of other people.

Three Key Elements

Element One

In Creative Visualization's first element, it states that you must "desire whatever that something is that you want to visualize and manifest." While I say, you must "have clarity of what you want to Accomplish." Both are about knowing what you want to realize from the start. Just as you had to be clear about what you wanted to achieve when you wrote down your three accomplishments, it is the same with your visualization. Before you begin, ask yourself, "What do I want to create in this visualization?"

Element Two

Gawain's second element is that "you must have belief" while I say, "you must believe." While belief may be something you have, believing is the process and the actions behind the belief. It's just a different way to do it (tomayto, tomahto). I chose this difference in language because, in my opinion, to believe in something requires more action behind it and, therefore, feels more powerful than having belief in it.

Element Three

According to Creative Visualization, the third element is that you must be able to "accept" it. While The Quinn Essentials version of acceptance is that you must be able to (yes, you guessed it) "receive" it. (Because what do we as women do? We Receive to Create!)

So, in review, the three key elements to the Creative Visualization original process is Desire, Belief, Accept and The Quinn Essentials process is Clarity, Believe, Receive. I would ask you to use The Quinn Essentials language in relation to the tools and this book.

Next, I am going to share the five steps to creating your visualization again that I initially learned from Shakti Gawain with applying my own language. Remember, you can't do this wrong.

5 Steps to Creating Your Visualization

Step One
Set your accomplishment.

Step Two
Create a clear picture of it in your mind.

Step Three
Focus on it often.

Step Four
Believe you can have it.

Step Five
Open yourself to receive it.

Now, that we've discussed in the first part of this tool the elements and steps you need to create your visualization, you may be wondering what the next step is... This is where Shakti's work ends, and The Quinn Essentials tool begins. Get ready to bring your visualization to life.

What you do with your visualization next is one of the most powerful things you can do to support what you are creating. This is where I would like to introduce you to something called **Snippets** where we kick things up another notch and share the visualization with our people.

Snippets are small moments in time where you see something (in whichever way you personally "see" it) and bring in others to the process as you co-create the moment of what you want to happen. They are a small piece or brief extract of what you want to create.

The most important thing is that you ask people to see it for you. You share your snippet out loud or in writing with people who want the best for you. I don't believe we should keep our dreams or visualizations to ourselves. When you share them, they become more powerful because the more energy you can put towards your visualizations, the faster they happen.

I'm going to show you right now what a snippet is by creating one here, inviting you into my life for a moment, and "ask you to see something for me."

Andrea's Snippet

It's a beautiful February Saturday afternoon in Los Angeles. The weather is just perfect. It's not too hot; it's not too cold. I'm on my way to my first live women's Quinn Essentials workshop since 2020. I'm expecting 150 women. Most of them, I do not know. I'm having a really good hair day and I'm wearing this really fun navy outfit. I feel very comfortable moving around and stretching getting ready for a long weekend. I don't sit when I'm teaching the weekend workshops so getting my energy up is

important. I am ready to do this and can feel the butterflies in my stomach.

We're in this beautiful space and it's big and it's light. All my friends are there and they're so excited for me. My husband is there. My mom, Lovie, has come to visit and everybody's waiting for day one and I have several volunteers ready to help. We begin to see the women lining up to come in from outside and I'm getting more and more excited. My friend Nora says to me, "You go sit in the back and go receive." I'm now sitting in the back smiling ear to ear seeing that women are all gathering safely, and we are about to embark on something that hasn't taken place in a long time.

Let me take you quickly to the end of the day, where everybody's just left feeling great, and they'll be back tomorrow for the second day. Oh, my God! We are all buzzing! My friends are coming out of the back, laughing with champagne. My husband is smiling. We are all so excited because we know that we have started to create the live events that women are craving. I am so grateful to have that magical experience today.

That's my snippet.

Were you there? What did you see? Could you feel it in your body? Maybe your stomach started getting tingly. Did you smile? Was your heart racing? Did you see something that I didn't include here?

That was a Snippet. I just launched my snippet, and you came along with me. I put my dream in your hands. We all went there together and by doing that, we launched it! Did you notice it was very condensed and not too long? They are not dissertations; they are moments in time you want to create and share as a tool to accomplish your dreams. Our combined energies become even more powerful than if I had just imagined it alone. (And thank you for sending me good energy so that I can receive it.)

Whatever we focus on is what we will bring into our lives.

I notice what happens to women is that we so often keep our dreams to ourselves. We're afraid of being judged and so we hold things back based on not knowing who to trust. I get that. But the great news is that you've now begun to identify who your people are. Now, when you sit with a group of women who are your people and launch your dreams with them, things will begin to change for you in such a big way.

I've been doing this for so long that my mom, Lovie, is now fully trained in Snippets. When something comes up, I'll call her and say, "Hi, mom. I need you to see something for me." And she'll stop what she's doing.

Then I'll say, "Okay, mom, but here's the deal – remember, no comments." She'll say, "Okay, I'm ready." Then I tell her what it is. She always responds with, "I see it for you, honey." And I'll say, "Thanks, mom. I gotta go. Bye!" and hang up the phone. That's all I'll need.

She's not the only one. My best friends are all pros at Snippets too. We live all over; from Los Angeles, New York, San Francisco to Switzerland but we are all on one Snippet chain. Someone will write, "Hey guys, it's me in New York. I'm up for a big promotion. I'm going in. I need you guys to see this for me." My first question is always, "What are you wearing?" Why do I need to know what she's wearing? Because then I can see her more fully and it adds that much more energy to the launch.

She'll get as specific as possible and now because I tried to get as specific as I can, I'm right there with her. Next thing, we'll get a text from San Francisco. "I see this for you." A couple of hours later, Switzerland wakes up. "I see it, you got it." Everybody's doing it, we're on it together and we're all there with her. We don't tell her what her accomplishment should be or how she should achieve it, that's for her to launch, but we will share any additional details of what we see as we envision it.

You don't realize it, but you do this all the time, just with the wrong intentions. So often we sit around with our friends, we whine (or wine) and we complain about all that is going wrong. And then we don't understand why things aren't changing in our lives. It's because we're launching this precious creative energy into the negative! Instead of focusing on what we are looking to create, we talk about how bad our ex-husbands are or how bad the job market is or how bad politics are right now.

This is such an important distinction to make. Whatever we are focusing on is what we will bring into our lives. Now when you sit there with your friends, instead of focusing on all the negative things you want to change, teach them this process and begin to focus on all the amazing things you are bringing into your lives.

Success Story #1

I'd like to share with you a story about a very well-known Financial Coach within The Quinn Essentials community. At the time, she was in her late 40s and previously only had one boyfriend when she was in her 20s. She had never lived with anyone and wanted love in her life but felt like relationships weren't as big a priority as they used to be. On the night the ladies shared their snippets with one another in class, she had come in to create a snippet around the expansion of her new business model, not love.

As she got up to do her Snippet, something inside her told her to create one for love. She became taken aback by what she was hearing within herself but since she was now getting in the habit of listening to herself (thank you Tool #3), she knew she needed to share a Snippet on love. She even admitted to arguing with herself and saying things like, "Yeah, like that's ever going to happen for me." But ultimately, she listened.

She sat down in front of the group and told us, "This is not what I planned to talk about, ladies. It's my second time taking this workshop and doing this process. I thought I was going to talk about the expansion of my business, but this time I'm going to have to talk about love."

She then began to talk about meeting a man.

Oh, my God! We could see it, we could feel it and we could see him. We all said, "I see him. He has a lot of energy with a big smile. He's got black and silver, salt and pepper hair." So many women yelled out things they saw for her and so many of us saw the same thing!

We saw it so intensely that we were freaking out. By the way, she had also just had surgery on her ankle and the doctors thought she may walk with a limp for the rest of her life. But woman after woman said that they saw this man for her and in their version of her Snippet, we all saw that she was walking with him limp-free.

A few months later, she met Frank who fit our description to a T! A few years after that, I had the great joy of being a guest at their wedding. As she walked down the aisle to join this wonderful man, there wasn't even the slightest limp to her walk. Talk about dreams coming true!

Can you see how when something inside of her said, "talk about love," she listened? This energy is magic. Stop hiding your dreams and stop feeling embarrassed about them. Listen to them. Share them with your people. To this day, she gives credit to that night for all the women who helped her to create the energy behind manifesting her visualization.

Specificity is key in launching your Snippets.

We've had women in the workshop who want to find the love of their life. They sit in our groups and together they create a visualization of a wedding with someone they haven't even met yet. But they get as specific as they can, and it is the most profound thing.

Listening to them, we are all moved to tears. And time after time, I will get an email six months after the workshop that reads, "I've met him! It's amazing." Or "We're already running off and getting married."

Another woman who was in my workshop had decided that one of her accomplishments was to find love. She was in her late thirties, had been born in Paris, went to school in France, but had come to America and had lived here for most of her life after school. She had also listened to herself and knew that she was going to move back to Paris to find love. So, she packed up everything, bought her one-way ticket to Paris, and the last night of our workshop was also going to be her last night in Los Angeles.

When that night came, she decided that in order for her Snippet to be authentic and specific, she had to share it with us in French. Specificity is key in launching a Snippet.

She closed her eyes and began to speak. She described meeting the love of her life in Paris for the first time, having an almost instant connection, and knowing that he was the one for her. She was living that moment so deeply that, suddenly, tears began to stream down her face. Even though we couldn't understand all the words she was saying, we knew the meaning behind them, and we knew that she was feeling this future so deeply it was as if she was experiencing it in front of us. We were all a mess. Our heads were down and eyes closed. Our hearts were in it and we were sobbing.

Even if we didn't speak French, we all knew. We were all there with her. It was a profound moment for everyone.

When you share in someone's Snippet, you will never forget that moment you spent in her life, EVER.

I have heard some women say, "I'm so painfully shy." I say to them, "I get that. Close your eyes and let's do this anyway." Once they've done it, they will tell me that sharing their vision with other women who offer so much support (sometimes more support than they've had in their entire life) is one of the greatest experiences that's ever happened to them. When you share in someone's Snippet, you will never forget that moment you spent in her life, ever. You may not remember her name from the workshop, but you will often think, "Oh, I wonder if she received her snippet? I hope she's doing well. I hope she's great." Suddenly, you're sending that beautiful energy to her once again, regardless of where she is in the world.

Sharing Snippets has taken on a life of its own within The Quinn Essentials community and we're currently in the process of starting an organization that's focus is about sharing Snippets from women all over the world. It is important we visualize the desires and dreams of women and support them. If you want it, I want it for you.

Success Story #2

One of the women who took this class in 2009 was a successful publicist in Hollywood. We even joked that she was such a big deal that she had her own parking spot with her name on it. When she took this class, she knew that she needed to accomplish her dream of leaving Hollywood behind and becoming a nurse so that she could work with children in pediatric oncology. This had been her dream since she was a little girl. Now 34 years old, she had decided to go into nursing school even though she would be the second oldest person in her class. But that wasn't going to stop her.

In the Snippet she shared with us, she was using her vacation time to travel to Africa; working with Doctors Without Borders to give vaccines to children. (To this day, I will run into someone who was there that night, and they will tear up remembering her Snippet and what a huge shift it was.)

A few years went by, she was near the end of her time in nursing school and nervous about what would be coming next for her. So, I told her to email her snippet to the community of women who had taken the workshops!

At first, she said she couldn't do it. She was too shy. I told her I knew she could. (This is how things shift, ladies. Trust your people!) She agreed. But then I had my Ask. I told her I would love to receive her telling others her experience of sharing her snippet. So, she sent a letter to the community of women explaining what she wanted us to see for her and then she gave us her snippet.

As promised, this is the letter of her sharing her experience:

"To the amazing power that is this group,

When I sent my first Snippet to the group, Andrea had to so talk me into it. I don't know why I was feeling shy about sending it, but I was. But I got over it and sent it.

Seriously, 10 minutes later, I got my first response from a woman who was seeing my Snippet and sending me all the love, light and energy that she could. By the next morning, I had even more responses echoing the same. The feeling that came over me is a little hard to describe. I just felt so supported and cared for and looked out for by people who didn't even know me. These words that these amazing women took the time to send to me meant more than I could have ever imagined. It was so very powerful and empowering. I felt that no matter what the outcome with my Snippet, that it would all be okay. And that I had love and support coming from a place that I'd never really known existed before.

These women in this special and unique group give me permission. I'm in a constant practice of the nine tools of The Quinn Essentials. They're slippery suckers sometimes. But this week, I think I nailed the Ask.

With tons of love and even more gratitude.

This is the email Snippet I sent that went out to all the women in the community in 2010:

'Yikes, this is my first Snippet. Guess I'm finally ready to ask for as much love, light and positive energy you can send my way for something I care so much about. I'm trying to get into UCLA pediatric oncology unit to do my final preceptorship for nursing school. This is where I want to be, and now I'm just waiting on the administration to see if it can happen.'

'Here's the snippet that I would love for you all to see for me:

There I am, wearing my light blue UCLA scrubs, and comfy Nikes, all set for my first day on the peds oncology floor. I walk into UCLA Mattel Children's Hospital, and I'm greeted by an *enthusiastic preceptor who can't wait to teach me all she knows. We get reports at 7:00 AM from the night shift nurses and begin what will be an amazing first day. I have the privilege of helping my preceptor take care of incredible kids who are all responding really well to chemo. I'm charting, hanging IVs, giving meds, researching treatments, listening to parents, answering concern questions from patients, and celebrating good test results.*

My first 12-hour shift is more than I could have asked for and day one leaves me with more fulfillment, inspiration, and feelings of knowingness than I could have ever in my wildest dreams imagined.

Thank you for letting me share this with you. It means a lot that I could send it out.'''

Now that you've heard so many of these stories, it may be no surprise to you that she, in fact, became a nurse at the UCLA Oncology Department for Children and has been there for years now.

Do you see the power of this? While you were reading her letter, couldn't you envision what she was saying exactly? Couldn't you see her little blue outfit and her little Nikes? This is the magic of what happens when you stop talking about the things you don't want to be living and, instead, teach this to your friends and launch your dreams with the people who care about you.

Imagine a world where we meet up, create a snippet party by zoom, go to dinner or call up our friends and we all talk about our dreams and what we wish for each other. No gossiping about other people. No chatting about how bad something's been. Instead, launching snippet after snippet. It's that powerful! I've even had women come and take my Quinn Essentials workshop because their friends taught them Snippets and they said, "I've got to do this workshop because I've got to learn more about how to do this since my friends' dreams are coming true."

Stop hiding your visualizations.
Share them with your people.

I want to share with you one more success story to magnify the importance of the visualization process. When you start to do this, it is like nothing you will ever experience. It will stay in your heart for the rest of your life. You will see things. You will know that there are people who are launching this for you just like you are launching it for them.

Success Story #3

In one workshop, we had a woman who was taking the course for the second time. She had received the manifestation of her first snippet as well as accomplishments and wanted to come back for a refresher since she was ready to create more magic. When it was time for her Snippet, she suddenly sat in front of everyone, started crying and blurted out, "I can't."

I said, *"What do you mean you can't? You've done this before."*

"I can't. I just can't; it's too painful."

"Okay," I said, "Just say what you can. You don't have to do a whole Snippet."

She agreed to do a very small Snippet and told us, "I'm sitting in my bed and it's a beautiful day and it's warm and I'm holding a baby."

She put her head down and she started to cry, "That's all I can do. I can't do any more."

With open hearts, everybody in the workshop instantly piped up in support of her vision and began to share with her what they saw. One side of the room yelled out that they saw a girl. The other side said, "No way! It's a boy!" They were arguing with each other over this baby and, meanwhile, she was so afraid that she was never going to be able to get pregnant.

At this time, our Quinn Essentials Accomplishment Workshops met once a month. So, by the time we got to the last class, it had been a couple of months since that night.

Can you guess what happened? She showed up to the last class pregnant. With twins. One boy. And one girl.

Her fears about becoming pregnant were so real to her that she could not get past them, but that night with the support of a room full of women, she found the courage and the belief that she could receive it. It was a night I will never forget.

Again, one of the most important things about your visualizations and snippets is that you must make sure you are sharing them with people who want the best for you. Absolutely protect them from the people in your life who you know are not-your-people. Please do not share this with those people in your life who always say, "Why would you want to do that?"

Honor each individual dream. You can do it every day. You can align with something you want to accomplish by telling the story of what you want someone who has your best interest at heart to see for you. You can do this as often as you like. Don't dilute it. Know that this isn't your one chance – this is your first one. You can have as many visualizations as you would like.

Importantly, it's got to feel real. Your feelings and thoughts create everything in your life. You've got to be able to really be there because this is real. We're dealing with magic, grab your wand kind of stuff. Honor that magic inside of you. If you can't do it right away or are struggling with the process, please read *CREATIVE VISUALIZATION* BY SHAKTI GAWAIN for inspiration. It's a small little book and the perfect thing to pick up for a weekend read.

Another key point to visualizing is not to become attached to the Snippet turning out the exact way you see it. Remember earlier in the chapter when I shared my snippet? Maybe my workshop won't happen in February. Maybe there will be less or more women. Maybe it will be a cloudy day instead of sunny. But the point is to continue to see it and then let the Universe do its thing. As I have said before, I believe the Universe is always working on our behalf and things can turn out better than we can even imagine. Haven't you ever imagined something in your life and then in the future, it happened? You created it. This is how powerful we are.

When you wake up in the morning, know what you'd love to Receive and see your Snippet in your mind. (Are you starting to see how these tools all support each other?!) Get up, do your stuff, let it come in and out of your thoughts all day. (You are going to think about something all day, why not the dream you are creating.) Go down and pick up the mail, think about it again. See it in your mind while you're cooking dinner or commuting home from work.

Send your best friends a text that says, "Hey guys, I would really love you to see this for me." Engage in how powerful it is not only to visualize the life you want but include the people in your life to help you to make it happen. Teach Snippets to your friends. Teach it to your mates. Teach it to your children. The more humans who engage together in powerful creations, the better it is for our world.

Visualizations don't have to be perfect. They just need to have the intention and thought behind them to help you manifest what you want to accomplish.

Clearly see it, believe it, now get ready to receive it.

Tools in Motion

1. Read *Creative Visualization* by Shakti Gawain.

2. Create your visualization based on what you want to accomplish then create a Snippet.

3. Keep seeing your snippet or snippets as often as you want.

4. Share your snippet with your people. Start with "Would you see this for me?"

5. Teach the Snippet process to your family and friends and have a snippet party.

Good to Know

1. There is no wrong way to visualize.

2. Whatever we focus on is what we will bring into our lives.

3. Specificity is key in launching your Snippets.

4. When you share in someone's Snippet, you will never forget that moment you spent in her life, EVER.

5. Stop hiding your visualizations. Share them with your people.

Continuing the Conversation

Please join me for a video which will assist you in visualizing and creating your snippet.

http://www.thequinnessentials.com/visualize/

or scan QR code

Chapter VIII
EMPOWER YOUR WORD

Q

You're living the life you are talking about.

In the first four tools, you learned the key components for your inner life: The importance of Receiving and with your I AMs, the power of knowing who you are at the soul level. We then discussed how you must be able to Listen as well as having Self-Acceptance in order to achieve your dreams. For your life out in the world, you've seen how the tools to accomplishing your dreams begin when you Connect, have the courage to Ask, and understand the importance of both Visualizing and sharing it with others so that they can aid you in accomplishing all that you want to bring into your life. And now with Tool Number Eight, the fourth and final tool to use out in the world, you must EMPOWER YOUR WORD.

I want you to put your hands on your throat for just a second and make the sound, "Mmmmm..."

Do you feel that vibration? Everything is in that vibration because vibration is creation. We are atoms and molecules, protons, neutrons, and electrons that all vibrate. (See, I did listen in seventh grade science class!) In fact, we are all vibrating right now and it is this vibration that creates the life you have. You are living the life you've been talking about and what you say now will create the life you will have. If you talk about how receiving that promotion will never happen for you, it won't. If you have found yourself saying, "Well, I'm over 40, and it's going to be easier for me to get hit by a bus than find love," then you will probably remain single.

Everything happens from speech. In the Bible, it says, "In the beginning there was the Word, and the word was God." (John 1:1) But it's not just in the Bible. Every great culture, religion, nationality, and language has something to say about the word. In Wicca, the pagan religion before Christianity, the high priestesses said, "Your word is your wand." In the Jewish language of Yiddish, there is the saying, "From your mouth to God's ears." Even the biggest naysayers in the world will often say something like, "Be careful what you wish for" because they know if you say it, it's probably going to happen.

When you Empower your Word, there is an energetic shift that happens almost immediately in your life. When you talk with confidence and gratitude, it is like a beacon of light that attracts better situations, people and more success. Talking with confidence is a very hard thing for women since they feel they will be judged or seen as arrogant, but to be honest, people actually feel safer in the presence of a confident woman. (And if they don't, they are not-your-people.)

The power is in the words themselves.

One of the things I am clear about is that you must know how to talk about yourself and what you are looking to accomplish with respect and honor. It's your belief about your life that creates your life. How are you talking about what you want to accomplish? Are you speaking with a defeatist attitude? Are you locked into telling stories of what hasn't happened for you, instead of what has already manifested? We all have bad days and don't feel like speaking powerfully when we are not feeling it. I get it. So, during those times, I opt for the old saying "If you have nothing nice (or powerful) to say, don't say anything." (Even to yourself.)

There is so much power in the spoken word that there are countless books written about creation and the word. I know women can be very hard on themselves (hopefully Tool #4 Self-Acceptance is helping you with that) and we are habitually speaking with words that disempower ourselves. No one taught us to speak with self-respect so, in order to do so, we quite literally have to practice it. To do that, you must create scenarios in which you practice what is known as an old-fashioned "elevator pitch."

An elevator pitch is a term defined as using a brief, persuasive speech that you use to spark interest in what you do. Many salespeople are familiar with this term. What would happen if, at the next place you showed up, the person who can help you receive your accomplishments asks you about it? What if they ask you to describe the type of business you want to open or the type of love relationship you are wanting to find? Can you in this moment speak about it with power? If not, you must practice.

This is where the first four tools can really help. If you are open to receiving, speak about yourself using your I AMs, be present to Listening and are accessing Self-Acceptance, then your elevator pitch should be amazing!

Later, in this chapter's Tools in Motion, I will ask you to do a little bit of role playing. You're going to write out your elevator pitch introducing yourself to 'whoever' you are meeting who can help you with your accomplishments. If you want to find love, then don't talk about all the ways you've been done wrong. The proper way would be to mention what you are looking to receive in the way of a loving partner. Again, give them your I AMs because that is the mirror to yourself you will need to find and then list some requirements as they apply to relationships. Believe me; you will sound confident, powerful, and not bitter.

Success Story #1

During one workshop where we were reviewing this tool, one of the ladies in the class said that she had an announcement to make. She said, "I want to use this opportunity to Empower my Word by letting all of you know that I will be hosting a cabaret and donating the money to Children's Hospital. I am an AMAZING singer and since I, myself, have recently recovered

from cancer, I want to give back and make a difference." We were so excited for her. She asked if we would all help sell tickets so she could "sell out" and make this event a success. We all yelled "Yes!" When we all invited people to come, we told them that there was this AMAZING singer who wanted to do a cabaret for Children's Hospital and with the effort of the ladies in the class she "sold out" the dinner theater. It was opening night and all the women in her workshop including myself were sitting waiting for the curtain to come up. Suddenly one of the women asked, "Has anyone heard her sing?" In that moment, we realized no one had heard her sing! Everyone's eyes opened wide as we didn't think to hear her sing beforehand. One of the women spoke up and said, "Well she said she was AMAZING so confidently that I didn't even think to ask."

It was curtain time and with anticipation and fingers crossed (to be honest) her first song began. She was absolutely AMAZING just like she said, and we all laughed and cried because of what she was doing and how wonderful it was to trust a woman when she tells you she's AMAZING.

People are not used to a woman being powerful in how she speaks about herself. We wait for her to be humble and not too big. This story is what happens when women absolutely believe in themselves. When you believe in you, the world will believe in you.

Women must be able to articulate the wonderful things that make them unique.

Let's say you are a gifted therapist. Why would I want to see you? In every profession, there are plenty of therapists but what makes you unique? That is what this tool is all about. If you were to speak powerfully about yourself, what would you say? In those moments when people ask you what makes you different or why do you charge so much or why do you think you want this money, you must be able to tell them in no uncertain terms who you are.

In describing yourself, create your elevator pitch by relating your experience of you. Going back to the therapist example, the last thing you should do is describe the benefits of therapy. They want to hear about YOU.

Now, I'm going to model for you how I talk about me and my business. Let's say I go to a gathering and someone says, "So, I hear you're a life coach." And then maybe their next sentence is something along the lines of, "Isn't everyone a life coach now?"

Here's how I respond, *"Yes, and there are over seven billion people in the world. Everyone needs one so we actually need more coaches."* (I never take offense to somebody saying that because I know they're probably nervous to talk to me and don't know what to say.)

Don't get offended because of what someone else might say or question about you. This can especially happen when we're venturing into something that the other person may not understand. For example, if you're an actor, someone may say something along the lines of, "So, you're an actor? Good luck in this town." (Here's where we begin to see that so often people say things because they're not sure how else to respond.) So now, instead of looking to be offended, you can stand in your power and say, "Yes, I am an actor and thank you."

I get this question all the time too. "Why do you have such a long waiting list? Tell me, what makes you different?"

Again, it's not my job to educate them on life coaching. It's my job to speak powerfully with respect for myself and my career. *My answer is usually something like this: "Well, I have to be honest. I believe that I'm the greatest mirror holder in this town. I see people before they do. I have super strong arms and I will hold a mirror in front of them for as long as it takes. And when they finally see who they really are, my job is done. I also feel that it's the Universe's way of giving me the best friends I'll ever have in a lifetime. Because it's so intimate and we are so connected that I know I'll know them forever. Usually the problem in someone's life is that they have forgotten who they are and need to look in the mirror and remember."*

Some people will look at me confused. When they do that, I know they don't get me and probably won't be a client in the future. Others will look at me and ask me, "Do you have a card?" Because they get it, they get my language, and they understand wanting to remember their greatness.

And do you know how I came up with that?

I realized I had to get to know myself. I had to really sit with myself and ask, "Who is Andrea Quinn?" Because Andrea Quinn is who I must talk about with power.

I came to the "mirror" example because I love Disney. I mean I *really* love Disney. It's women in adversity, overcoming all the obstacles and then they get to live happily ever after. What?!? It's amazing. And there's magic, too! All the stuff the female character has done wrong, everyone she has run away from, everything she has destroyed is forgiven and it's all about love in the end. Why wouldn't I love that? It's Happily Ever After.

I asked myself, "Okay, Andrea, you love Disney. What is it in those stories that can articulate what you do for a client?" I thought about it and realized it's the "magic mirror"! That's what I love. So, I'm going to hold that space for people until they see they are "The Most Powerful One of All" in their own lives and that they already have everything they need to make their dreams come true.

How couldn't I describe myself like that? This is what I had to do. I had to get to know Andrea and what Andrea loved. I had to tell them my experience of the coaching experience in first person. I can't tell anyone who's asking about the experience my clients have; I can only share my own. And when I do it with respect and honor, I am not only empowering my presence, I am also empowering my practice.

You must get in front of people and powerfully tell them about you and your experience of you. What's your experience of who you are in a love relationship? (If you want to be fixed up with a future partner.) What's your experience of the business you are pitching? (If you are looking for funding.) What's your experience about fashion? (If you want a job in that field.) See where we are going? Whatever it is for you, get connected and clear about how you experience it so that you can share this knowledge about yourself with others using the most powerful words.

Another important point to empowering your word is if you can't talk about yourself powerfully, then others can't talk about you powerfully either. My clients know how to talk about me, "You have got to go see Andrea. I can't explain what she does in our session, but she sees me. I know that for sure." That's another way of saying I'm their magic mirror. I see them. I see you. That's what goes on in there, they are seen. In my opinion, this is what makes me unique. (Again, in my opinion, which is the only opinion that should matter to me.)

Words are energy.

I would like to share something with you that changed my way of speaking about myself in 2006. I was sent this by a friend, and she had said it was written by a minister, but she didn't know who had written it. For some reason, she thought I would like it and perhaps I needed this in my life. She was right! It was a very hard time in my family as my father was very ill at the time. I certainly wasn't speaking words of power and instantly became overwhelmed with gratitude when this teaching snapped me out of my funk.

The Spoken Word

You have within you the power to make your life what you desire it to be. Your spoken word is not only powerful to make changes in your life; it is the power through which definite changes come about. Regardless of outside influences, you shape your life through your thoughts and words. You do this whether or not you are aware of it.

When you know the power of words, especially your spoken words, you will put a guard at your lips and be very wise in what words pass through, just as you will do the same with your ears in that you will allow only that which is uplifting, positive and life-enriching to enter and find lodging in your thinking process.

Words can make your life miserable or marvelous; it is up to you. Just as what you think makes you what you are, words mold and shape your life because words are the expressions of thought, ideas held in mind. Negative words result in negative, unhappy experiences – positive words result in positive, happy and prospering experiences.

In speaking words, you are literally moving substance, making a definite difference somewhere in some way. Most of all, you are making a definite, although seemingly imperceptible, difference within yourself and upon the conditions of your life. To affirm something is to decree. You are decreeing something is so. Doing this with understanding faith is sure to result in satisfying experiences.

In 2009, *Time* magazine put the words "How Faith Can Heal" on the cover. It was the cover story about the power of prayer. The article inside discussed how there had been all different forms of research and "blind testing" conducted on people with the same illnesses. Those who were prayed for found that the cancer had begun to shrink. Again, "In speaking out loud or in your mind, you are literally moving substance, making a definite difference somewhere in some way."

These are the reasons why I tell people to be very careful about what and who they're talking about. I remind them that words are energy and that even when you are thinking them, they have an energetic form because, in your mind, you're still putting them into words.

We must be responsible for our speech. We must be diligent in this practice all the time. As women, we are very trained to talk about others; trained to talk about what we're angry about or how they've offended or wounded us. We talk about things in a negative way and wonder why our lives are not what we want them to be. Instead, we must talk about all the things we want to accomplish. I know it is really hard not to gossip. I get that. If I am not careful, I can get caught in the gossip trap as well. There are moments when it takes everything in me not to join in. I have friends who will say, "Well you know I love her, but..." They must start off nice. And then they go in with a "but..." And I start cracking up. When they say, "You know I love her, but..." I go, "No 'but,' stop there. I can't do this." It's not that I am perfect, it's just that I work these tools very hard in my own life. This tool keeps me on my toes for sure.

I'm very fortunate. I have a very blessed practice where successful people come to me from all walks of life. One time, when one of the biggest divorces in Hollywood went down, a lot of people knew I knew them. They knew that I'd known them for years and had gone to their house several times. People would come to me ready for gossip. They would say, "Can you believe so-and-so are getting a divorce? What's your opinion?" My response was always, "I don't want one."

"What do you mean, you don't want one? You mean you don't have one?"

"Oh yeah, I got one. But you know what my business is, my marriage, not theirs. I'm out. I don't want to talk about them."

Have you heard the saying that "gossip is like drinking poison waiting for the other person to die"? I work so hard empowering my word because I don't want to poison myself, my life or anyone else with gossip. Because, if I do, then I can't empower myself and create the life I want. I know this can be so hard for women. We are really good at tearing people down (including ourselves) with words and telling others what they did to us and how offended we are by them. We're great at that. But we must stay out of that trap because it will take you down. Instead of judging them and telling everyone we know about it, our job is to figure out the way to stay empowered with our words. When I get into that type of situation, I try to focus on the fact that there is contrast to everything and this just might be a "contrast moment" in my life.

The language we use in this Tool is so important. What do you say when someone asks you about someone who isn't your people? In the past, you may have been dragged down by gossip and negativity. Now, I want you to look at it from a place of, "She's not-my-people, I wish her well and hope she finds her people." Don't give it any of your precious energy! Can you see how much better that feels?

You no longer have to go into the drama. You can hold that space. Now that you've learned this language, it's like an off ramp from the negativity highway. Here's the truth. He or she's not-your-people, you're not their people, game over. Let's be done with it and not let it bring us down.

Remember what the Dalai Lama said? We've got a world to save! And we can't do our part playing small. If we are not careful with how we are speaking about ourselves, our work, and the world we are living in, it's going to cost us, big time. Again, remember that old saying, "If you have nothing nice to say, don't say anything at all." If you've been stuck doing it for so long and you don't know how to stop, then you've got to really work this tool.

If you feel like you're going to say something negative, try to release it without verbalizing it. Remind yourself as often as you need that negative talk just feeds our ego and it takes down our power. Instead, empower your words. Remember, no matter how smart you are, or how perceptive you may be, someone else's life is not about you. Just because you have an opinion doesn't mean you need to give it. That's their career, their marriage, their kids. Nobody's asking you (even if they are asking you), stay in your lane.

It's all about how we talk to ourselves.

Launch your dreams, talk about your wishes, acknowledge people's magnificence. This is power. This is where the tools all start coming together. And now, with Tool Number 8, we know we must Empower Our Word. We must be able to talk about and articulate our word in a way that respects and honors ourselves and that serves us as women, what we're creating and the projects, lives, and things that we want to accomplish. (Do you see how all of the tools are now beginning to work together?)

When you work these tools, they become a part of who you are. Go down your checklist before you go into your meetings or before you go in for that interview. Go down that list and remember how everything you are NOT is irrelevant. Everything you are and all that you do best is what you focus on.

Here's the truth. You've got to love being you because you're stuck with Her. You get up in the morning, you look in the mirror, and She is still there – every day. Everyone else is going to leave you someday in life; our lovers, our family members, our animals, they're all going to leave. But that one person who is going to keep staring at you every freaking day in the mirror is YOU. So, you'd better like Her, and you'd better be able to talk about Her in an empowered way.

I promise you that there's power in this work. When you work these Tools, they're going to become a part of you. What happens then is not only are you empowered but you're also going to be happy.

Take some time, reflect, and ask yourself how do you want to be spoken about? Ask yourself what you want to do and what your big dreams are. It doesn't happen overnight and it's something I still do. I log off from the rest of the world and sit with myself regularly. Just as I would want to invest my time with anyone else that I love, I want to invest time in an authentic relationship with myself. She deserves it. I'll ask her, "What's your favorite thing, Andrea?" And she'll remind me that it's "Happily Ever After."

Remember your business is you and the way you wield your words with power is paramount to success. From now on, if people don't support you in your vision, you've got to begin to shift the conversation from "They don't support me because my work isn't good" to "Oh, I'm speaking to people who aren't my people." If you have a bad meeting or you're an artist and they didn't buy your work, the key is to shift away from internal conversations like, "My art must suck because nobody has bought it." Or, "People don't buy my style of art anymore." Instead, shift your words to, "They weren't my people and when I find my people, they will buy my art."

It's all about how we talk to ourselves, how we talk about our lives, and if we use empowering or disempowering language.

Empowering your Words can change the world.

Now think about the news and, more specifically, negative news. This is something that does affect us all. I went on a news diet a while ago and I cut myself out of all of it. (Even the Dali Lama only listens to 30 minutes of news a day!)

Here's what I know, everybody's got an opinion. And so many of the people in the media exaggerate or adjust the truth in order to serve their own agendas, pulling you in to increase their ratings and sell more time to advertisers. That's across the board.

Unless I see it or hear it for myself, I'm going to assume that it's not 100% accurate. Knowing that is how I feel, I decided... BOOM! I'm done allowing the prefiltered information to come my way. (Words have power. Remember?) So, I am diligent about not only what I say but what I allow to be said to me and what I listen to.

Embrace the power of individuality. Refuse to go one way or the other just because someone tells you to. I understand that a lot of people want to talk about the situation in the world right now. But talking about this stuff all the time is what's taking us all down.

Here's what I want to hear... Are you ready?

I want to hear about your journey to your 'Happily Ever After.' I'm not sticking my head in the sand pretending that there aren't things in the world that need to be changed. Remember Tool #6, Ask? There are things we need to change now, and they need our attention. But, if I focus over there with all the pundits spinning their wares, I'm going to be pulled down into the muck. I've absolutely got to turn my head away from what I have no choice about and, instead, use my head to help in the areas where I can make a difference.

I know I have to turn away from that darkness and towards the light of what I know we can create to make the 'Happily Ever After' for the world happen. I'm not going down with them. This is why people are traumatized, this is why people are angry, this is why people are divided and this is why racism is at an all-time high right now. Because of all the craziness people are creating in the world with words.

Empowering your Words changes your vibration and your energy. Your words are so powerful and using them for the greater good will change not only your life but the world. It is perfectly fine not to agree with everyone, but it is not ok to use words of judgment that harm another human. I believe changing this world starts with changing how we speak and the words that we put out. This is power! This is truth! This is the Word!

Tools in Motion

1. Aligning with your Accomplishment list, create an elevator pitch to help you practice speaking with power.

2. Practice your elevator pitch as if you were talking to the person you want to meet. I also recommend practicing with a friend so they can help you with notes if your pitch needs to be stronger.

3. Take time every day to check in with yourself without distraction. Think about the words you are using to describe your day, yourself and your life. If it is disempowering, make a different choice in the moment.

4. Limit any negative words such as news, podcasts or any media where the light isn't leading the way. There are plenty of empowering things to read, listen to and learn from – find them.

Good To Know

1. The power is in the words themselves.

2. Women must be able to articulate the wonderful things that make them different.

3. Words are energy.

4. It's all about how we talk to ourselves.

5. Empowering your Words can change the world.

Continuing the Conversation

Watch this video to continue talking about Empowering Your Word.

http://www.thequinnessentials.com/empoweryourword/

or scan QR code

Section 3

Bringing It All Together

Chapter IX
LET GO

Giving up is Fear ~ Letting go is Faith.

Here we are. Arriving at Tool Number Nine. Ready? Drum roll, please...

LET GO!

LET GO!

LET GO, LADIES!

You must let go of doing it all, thinking it all, and controlling it all - LET GO! (Good. exhale.)

If "Receiving" is the In-breath, then "Let Go" is the Out-breath. As women, we tend to hold on too tightly to things in our life in an attempt to control everything. We fear that in letting go of our control, we will fail and lose all our power. We stop trusting and begin to manage every moment and situation based on things that have happened in our past. We keep an inventory of every painful experience and make sure to police our lives so that those painful experiences never happen again. This prevents us from receiving that exhale and Letting Go. (We even hold our breath all the time. Go ahead and exhale now please!)

As a self-proclaimed recovering control freak, I can tell you that one of the most important things about letting go is that you can only do it if you are present. In the present moment is the only place that you are truly powerful. When you are present, you are not attached to anything. The past is gone, the future isn't here yet and in the present moment, you are unattached to fear or judgment.

In the Introduction, I told you that the two tools that I personally work every day are Tool #1 (Receive) and Tool #9 (Let Go). Both tools really challenge me as a woman. I know that for me to be fully empowered, I must be present and aware of these tools every day in every situation of my life.

Letting go allows you to create ways to be present and this awareness keeps you in your power. You will find that fear does not have the control it once had in your past life. A great question to ask yourself is, "What is the truth in this very moment?"

When the corona virus was first introduced in 2020, for the first time in my life, the amount of fear in the world was palpable. The not knowing kept me spinning in the "What ifs." This is where I had to use this tool as if my life depended upon it and it did. Holding on to fear can lower your immune system and make you sick. I believe what we focus on and talk about is what we create. So, I took power back over my mind.

I turned off the media, began to meditate with guided meditations every day, started my gratitude journal again, listened to my gut and asked myself to start telling myself the truth. During that period, I didn't know what the truth was from the outside world and knew the only place I was safe with the truth was within myself.

When I asked, "What is the truth for you in this very moment?" I would say things like, "The truth is I am healthy." "The truth is in this moment, I have no virus." "I am grateful I have toilet paper." I made a conscious effort to take an exhale, let go in the moment and reconnect to Source. Literally that was a conversation I had with myself almost every day from March to August of 2020. This may not have been your experience with that period of time, but it was mine. Remember, during 2020, we all lived different realities with the virus but when I made the decision to let go and be present, it supported me through one of the darkest times in world history. I believe the art of letting go saved my mental health and my life.

You can let go of attaching to fear and practice talking to yourself about your present moments. Our mind can create worry about a future that hasn't come yet but if we are powerful enough, we can discipline our minds and overcome the habit of worry to let go to create the space to receive. It will take practice but if I can do it, you can do it.

To Let Go is to have Faith.

Letting go is another form of faith, specifically your faith. It is the act of trusting that while you may not know how it's going to happen, you do know, deep within, that life will unfold in the perfect way for you. Faith is the confidence in what we hope for and the knowing that the Universe, Source or God is working on our behalf even though we cannot see it.

There's no faith in giving up, is there? You can't be present while giving up. Giving up is fear and letting go is faith. Letting go of our attachment to a specific outcome and our attempts at controlling them is a major challenge for many women. That's why being in faith with a higher power is a co-creative endeavor that will make your life easier.

Trusting that you are always being supported in the highest good of your soul's journey by your spiritual guidance makes it much easier to let go. When we can let go of obsessively thinking about future outcomes and attempting to control how they will happen, we can be fully present in the moment. Letting go of outcomes is what brings us to the present moment allowing us to truly recognize opportunity. Often when someone is sad or anxious, it's because they are attached to some future outcome, judging from the past and over thinking it. When you accept that you are not in control of outcomes and, instead, consciously give the outcomes to spirit, energy, or whatever it is that works for you, then there is no longer any need to obsess about them. By being present in the moment, you can now connect to yourself and really tune into your feelings. This is why you must listen and, especially, you must listen to what you require. You can't do that if your head is full of fear, because when we are in fear, we'll only spiral into need.

The past is gone; the future isn't here yet. So, for you to let go of a situation, you must practice faith in the moment. Remember, when you are present, you are empowered. It's when we're somewhere else other than here, that is the problem. If you're basing your new businesses or new love relationships on fears or self-perceived failures of the things you have done before, you're not going to be as successful or joyful. I've asked some women who started their own businesses, "What empowered you to start your first business when you did?" They've almost always replied, "I don't know, I just did it. I didn't worry at that time about failing. I just knew I had to do it."

Isn't that interesting? It's because inherently when you start worrying about your next steps, it means you're trying to control everything. You begin thinking along the lines of, "It has to look like this" or "It has to be like this." And in that line of thinking, there's no room for the possibility of it being even greater than you can imagine. When we first start things, we must adopt what the Zen Buddhists call "A Beginner's Mind." The concept of "A Beginner's Mind" is defined as a positive attribute that refers to having an attitude of openness, eagerness, and lack of preconceptions when studying a subject, even when studying at an advanced level, just as a beginner would. In the beginner's mind, there are no attachments. The revered Zen teacher Shunryu

Suzuki says the following, "In the beginner's mind there are many possibilities, but in the expert's there are few."

I love to ask women, "In starting your life over, why don't you just do what you did the first time? Just start doing it, without fear of failure and if you don't like it, you can change it." (I get so much resistance from women when I ask this question.)

After a certain age or certain number of unsuccessful attempts, we begin to control with a tight grip to the point of hurting ourselves. You are going to make a big mistake by holding on to what you think it has to look like instead of being open to what could be as soon as you just let go. What you create in letting go is space. You create space for more things to come in for you to receive. You can't receive anything holding on; holding to your memories, holding to your fears, holding to what you think you know. When we keep asking questions like, "How is it ever going to happen," we have tunnel vision. Guess what... That's exactly why it's not happening. It's not happening because you're holding so tightly to the attachment you have in your head. Through this holding, you're not open to let the energy come in.

Looking at the previous 8 tools, you will have done all you could to accomplish your dreams. You will have opened yourself to **Receive**, standing on a foundation of your **I AMs**. You will have **Listened,** engaged in **Self-Acceptance**, **Connected, Asked, Visualized** and then **Empowered Your Word**. What else can you do? You've done everything within your power, now **Let Go**!

This is why I don't like speaking about things in terms of "goals." When you set goals, which I find masculine, you begin attaching to outcomes and you focus on the goals themselves, not the space around the goals. Remember, when you use the expansive term "accomplishments," you create a space around what you are wanting to create. By letting go of our attachments, plans, or 'have-to's, we create the space in our lives to receive. You can't receive if you are attached and refuse to Let Go. Not letting go of our worries, painful experiences, opinions, and judgments keeps us in a cycle of attachment where faith cannot live. Holding on looks like the following conversations you begin to have with yourself and others:

"I have a goal. I need to be married by the time I'm X."

"I'm too old to start again."

"I must be married a second time by the time I'm Y."

"I must have a baby by X or it's never going to happen for me."

"If I don't make this business work this time, I'm done."

"I will never trust in a love relationship again."

"I'm aged out in my industry and there is no way I will find the money or position again after my layoff"

Meanwhile, it's exactly these attachments and conversations that have been stressing you out.

Letting go doesn't mean giving up.

When we don't know "how" things will happen, we begin to hold on tightly to the plans we've created in our heads. We can miss the unexpected opportunities that can show up for us out in the world. "How" is the ego's way to keep us back. A lot of women won't move forward until they know "how" it will happen. "How" keeps us attached. Stay out of that trap! People can tell you "How" they got there once they've arrived, but no one knows "how" they are going to do anything when they start. Everything starts with the first step. Therefore, we must let go of these timelines we put on ourselves. I have a friend who had her second baby at 46, naturally. Yes, you read that correctly. After many years, she let go and it happened for her at 46. Letting go does not mean giving up.

There's all this worry that it must look like "this" or it has to be like "that" and when we keep asking questions like, "How's it ever going to happen?" We have tunnel vision. Guess what... That's exactly why it's not happening. It's not happening because you're holding so tightly and are attached to the story in your head. Through this holding, you're not open to let energy come in.

Have you ever had a situation where it turned out better than you thought it could? That's because you had to let go in order to get there! Or have you seen how for most people, it's exactly right at the moment when they stop doing something that it happens for them? That happens a lot for actors. They'll say, "I'm done. I'm done not planning a vacation and waiting for the next audition to come in. I'm done putting my life on hold. I'm out." And then they'll go on vacation. Suddenly the messages come in. "How are you? Where are you? We need you to make a video and film your audition. You're going straight to producers..." Coincidence? No. It's just how it happens when we Let Go and get out of the Universe's way.

How about the stories we hear of people who adopt a baby and then, suddenly, they're pregnant? That is so often part of the "letting go and having faith" process. These are things we weren't taught. Instead, letting go was something we were told not to do. How often have you heard the refrain, "Keep your eye on the ball." I hate that one. You know why? Because if I keep my eye only on the ball, then I'm going to miss the whole game. Instead, I want to invite you to use a new refrain, "Today I receive and I will let go." What keeps you stuck in anxiety, depression, fear, anger or even emptiness is when you're attached to something, some idea or some perceived outcome. It's when you are not only trying to control those things, but you are also asking yourself questions about your life with judgment and fear. (Does that sound familiar?)

Going back to your list of what you want to accomplish, I have some questions for you. "What one thing can you let go of that would allow you to take the first step in what you want to create?" "What story can you let go of that is keeping you from healing?" "What could your life look like if you let go?" These are powerful questions to ponder on the road to empowerment.

Again, we must practice letting go. Because being attached to controlling our outcomes does what? Keeps us from being present in this moment with our feelings and experience. (Are you starting to really feel this yet?) When you're not present with your feelings, you also aren't able to know when you're behaving in ways that are harmful to you. If you're not letting go and you are holding on, you're not present to knowing or seeing that what you're doing isn't in your best interest.

Remind yourself, why waste any more of your life trying to command the future as you think it should happen when you can't possibly control it anyway?

Life is right now in this very moment. Let that sink in. Maybe even read it again. Life is right now in this very moment.

Success Story #1

I had the pleasure of having a well-known choreographer take my workshop a few times. She has choreographed and danced all over the world with well-known artists like Prince, Britney Spears and many more. She is a hardworking, kind woman who is always taking care of her family and friends with so much love. Besides being a great dancer, she is also a rapper and singer and

decided it was time to create her first album. She wrote and recorded a demo dance song that was slated to be a hit and was being played at dance studios across the US. She also filmed a great video with a lot of her dance colleagues. The song was starting out a bit slow with downloads, but people had assured her these things take time and she needed to be patient.

Then life showed up.

Her family had one tragedy after another. She had a few unexpected funerals to attend and a lot of illnesses where she spent many days and nights in the hospital to support and advocate for her beloved family members. The timing could not have been worse for her career. She was just taking off with her music and to say she was frustrated is an understatement. With family always being her priority, she stopped promoting her music to take care of the members of her family who needed her. She took one final look at her song, it had only about 2,000 downloads so in that moment she decided to let go.

She told me that she knew what her priorities were and that she had faith that if this isn't her time to be in the music business, perhaps in the future, she would revisit it. As she said, "I turned my head away from the business and turned it towards my family." Eighteen months had passed since she even had time to dance let alone think of singing, but she never stopped believing in her path. She had said letting go in that moment was the *hardest thing she had ever done, but again it was her faith and love that kept her going. Then the miracle happened.*

Someone she hadn't seen in years texted her to congratulate her on how well her song was doing. She was very surprised, confused and taken aback. She thought to herself "They have it wrong." The next thing she did was look at her downloads and to her amazement, she had 1 million downloads from all over the world! She wasn't focusing on her music but, in her heart, she never gave up. She always thought she would do music again but with her family in such an upheaval, she made the right choice as she said, "For her Karma." It happened right at the perfect time when she was just about to get started again not only doing choreography but creating music.

"I didn't look at my music for 18 months and the timing for my song is better than it was before! Letting go was the best thing I did so that the Universe could deliver my song right on time." She had a big 1 million download party in Los Angeles, has reignited her career, and she is an example to many people on the art of Letting go. By the way, the title of her song is "Let It Go." Coincidence? I think not! (FYI not the Disney version.)

I am open to everything and attached to nothing.

If you look at the many spiritual teachers such as Buddha, they are always sitting with their palms up and hands open, not attached to anything. The only times their palms are touching are when they are in prayer. I have always found that interesting. We can see the same in so many of the images of Jesus that have been created. In them, he's standing or walking with his hands open. Images of the Goddess Kwan Yin also show her with open hands. She is said to have one thousand open hands, and, in those depictions, we see again non-attachment.

I'm going to tell you about a little saying from Wayne Dyer that I share with all my clients. I'd love you to say this out loud, over and over, in every situation you can. "I am open to everything and attached to nothing."

We attach to titles, we attach to identities, we attach to things when, meanwhile, we really need to be open and unattached to the things, which are only just constructs and limitations of what we can achieve. The moment you can become unattached, you are now free to be successful beyond what you can even imagine at this moment.

That's the difference, that's the power. I am open to everything and attached to nothing. If you can use this as a daily mantra or reflection, it will help you. I even had this written on my office chalkboard for a very long time to remind myself that as soon as I can let go, then I can receive and create all over again.

And, yes, we've all made mistakes. We've made big ones. What I tell people is, if you're going to mess up, make sure you mess it up in a big way. When you make a big mess, you tried in a big way. Make it so big that it leaves an impact. Because small messes, what's that about? If we're going to do this, let's just do it. We will only regret at the end of our lives the things we did not do.

I want you to know that I have made my fair share of big messes. I told you before how I was divorced and bankrupt before I could legally drink and before some of my friends had even gotten laid. (My nickname was Drama Quinn.) This stuff happens to women. I will never forget having to put a car out front of my apartment and let the bank take it. Looking back, I would have liked to have skipped those years between 19 and 30 if I could, but I wouldn't be who I am today without the life experiences to write this book.

I remember the day I figured out that if I was going to make a mess, then I was going to make a BIG one. Why be a wuss about it? At least I know that I've given it my all, and I've done something that I wanted to do in a big way. Because here's what I know, I'm a woman, I have choice, I have strength and I can start all over again.

One of the passages, again by Marianne Williamson in a *Return to Love*, was the game changer for me to let go. "*If you could have done it better, you would have.*" Wow! Read that again! "If you could have done it better, you would have!" You know that's truth and I hope it helps you Let Go the way it helped me.

Our job is to let go of all the things that we think, all the age restrictions, all the 'have-to's and 'should-have's – because we were doing the best we could at the time. (Take another exhale.)

Letting go is power.

Letting go is your connection to real power. It centers you. It makes you present. And in the present moment, when you are not in regret of your past mistakes or living in fear of making future mistakes, when you are in the moment, you are so powerful because that is when you know you can make good decisions. You can recognize your people. You can stand in what you require. But you can't do that with fear consuming your thoughts.

If letting go is something you're not good at, that's okay. It just means you'll have to get better at it. Like the other tools, it takes practice. First, start letting go of little things. Don't go right to that big thing you're having a hard time with. Start recognizing the little places where you can let go, try it out, and see how that feels. "Ooh, that's interesting." Or "Ooh, I never really liked going there. That's uncomfortable." Okay. Those are 'good-to-know's. When you start seeing what comes your way by releasing, you'll start trusting yourself more and more in the letting go process. Because it is a process. And once that happens, you can bit by bit, thing by thing, situation by situation, start applying it to those bigger parts of your life.

I work on releasing that energy in my meditations too. I know how important it is and how much it really helps. I remind myself that letting go makes me present. Being present is what brings success in. I recommend starting a meditation practice. There are many great apps and online mindfulness teachers to help you and it just takes as little as 20 minutes a day. I personally use Insight Timer, but there are many great apps out there.

Your amount of personal freedom is expanded by how much you will Let Go.

The character Holly Golightly portrayed by Audrey Hepburn in *Breakfast at Tiffany's* wonderfully represents letting go. She exemplified the art of being fabulous and being present. Being who she was and not making any excuses for it. There is a power in that type of personal freedom by letting go of your attachment to what others think of you. That's the whole thing, ladies, your own Self-Acceptance (Tool #4) is so important. Remember? Everybody else's approval doesn't matter. It comes second. If you like your art, sell it. If you're an actor and they're not hiring, create your own thing. Throw it out there and let people see you. If you're a coach, go help people. Stop waiting to reach an unattainable level. Let go of what you think and just take a step forward. What if you fail? Okay. But what if you don't? Did you think of that?

And I know it's really scary, especially around your children. Children are hard to let go of because you know so much better than they do. But in truth, we all have our own guides and angels and all of us are on a path, every one of us. You can only do it for them for so long. Eventually, you will always have to do what as a parent? Let go. You will have to let go in order to have a relationship with them as they get older. If we hold on too much and too tightly, we can't even breathe; nor can the people we're holding on to. (I learned that lesson with my nieces.)

Here is a beautiful poem by Rev. Safire Rose that I want to share with you. Take a deep breath, exhale, and read this poem slowly with intention. Listen to yourself say these words to yourself.

She Let Go

She let go.

She let go without a word. She let go.

She let go of fear.

She let go of the judgment.

She let go of the confluence of opinion swarming around her head.

She let go of the commitment of indecision within her.

She let go of all the right reasons.

Wholly and completely without hesitation or worry, she just let go.

She didn't ask anyone for advice, she didn't read a book on how to let go, she didn't search the scriptures, she just let go.

She let go of all the memories that held her back.

227

She let go of all the anxiety that kept her from moving forward.

She let go of the planning and all the calculations about how to do it just right.

She didn't promise to let go.

She didn't journal about it.

She didn't write the projected date in her Day-Timer.

She made no public announcement and put no ad in the paper.

She didn't check the weather report or read her daily horoscope.

She just let go.

She didn't analyze whether she should let go.

She didn't call her friends to discuss the matter.

She didn't do it in five spiritual minded steps.

She didn't call the prayer line.

She didn't utter one word. She just let go.

No one was around. When it happened, there was no applause or congratulations.

No one thanked her, or praised her.

No one noticed a thing.

Like a leaf falling from a tree, she just let go.

There was no effort, there was no struggle.

It wasn't good and it wasn't bad, it was just what it was.

It was just that.

In the space of letting go, she let it all be.

A small smile came over her face. A light breeze blew through her, and the sun and the moon shone forevermore.

Isn't that just beautiful? You don't have to take your stories with you anymore. You don't. They can be gone because you say so. You can let them go. The line that really got me was, *"Like a leaf falling from a tree, she just let go."* A tree doesn't think about it, it just does it with intuition and a connection to divine timing. Nature is our greatest teacher.

I believe whatever lesson you were meant to learn – I don't know if it's 10 years, 10 days, 40 years, 40 days, whatever it is – that experience showed up in your life right on time to teach you something. It is part of the growth of your soul. And the Universe (believe it or not) makes no mistakes. We're the ones who think we have all the control, but a bird sitting in a tree doesn't say, "So, anybody know where I'm supposed to fly to?" You think that's what they're saying? No. The birds align with the rhythm of nature and when the exact vibration hits, they know, "It's time to fly and where to go." And then they take off.

The flowers don't ask, "Is it time to bloom?" Even if there's a bunch of buds waiting to bloom. There's no "You go first. No, you go first. You can go. Are we supposed to open?" They each open right on time. There's a universal, beautiful vibration, and in that vibration, the first bud knows when to open for spring. And so does the next. Just like the first leaf of autumn knows when to fall.

All of us are animals. We are part of this beautiful Universe and everything else flows in rhythm, but us humans. We humans say, "I don't know. Is that what the Universe said? I'm not sure. I don't know, should I?" Yes! Yes, you should. Should you leave? Yep. Should you stay? Yep. Whatever it is. Just do it.

Let go of ex-boyfriends, ex-girlfriends, ex-lovers, ex-husbands and ex-jobs. Let go of that stuff that we're bringing with us, knowing that for whatever it is we release, what we bring in is going to be so much better. And it is going to be better. I promise.

Do you realize that every person in your life has shown up right on time? And guess what? They have left right on time too.

If the divorce was ugly, remind yourself that it's done. Even if you're still in the middle of it, what can you let go of that will make it easier? Sometimes you have that thing or situation where you thought, "Oh yeah, I let that go." Then a year later, something happens to pull you back in. We get surprised by the things that come back up in our lives and think, "Wow, I thought that I was done with this." Well, that's the time to go right into your toolkit. This is when you go, "Oh, okay, this one is a little deeper than I originally thought. What could I receive, so that I can really let go this time?" (Doesn't that type of question just feel good?)

Success Story #2

The last story I will be sharing in this book is one I personally witnessed for many years. In 2010, a woman who lived in Florida had taken this class several times and had a lot to let go of in the way of anger.

When she was younger, she decided she would get a whole body liposuction because she had lost a lot of weight and wanted to get rid of all the excess fat. She flew out of state to a top doctor in New York to do the procedure as he came highly recommended.

During the consult, she told him the area she was the most insecure about was her arms and how big arms were a thing in her family and she had already inherited them in her early 20s. He assured her that he knew what he was doing, and she would be very happy.

When she woke from her surgery, she was in a full body compression wrap except for her arms. She was confused and when he came in for a post-op visit, she asked him why her arms didn't need the wraps. The look on his face was one of shock and embarrassment as he forgot to do her arms!!! He apologized and told her it was a long surgery and to do her arms she would have to come back another time. Well, since she was from out of state, it wasn't that easy. To say she was angry is an understatement!

Years later in 2004, she was diagnosed with stage 3 breast cancer. Along with a double mastectomy and a lymph node removal, she got lymphedema in her right arm. Lymphedema is a swelling caused by abnormal accumulation of fluid since the lymph glands can't work efficiently. Her arms were even bigger! During the reconstruction surgery, the doctor had told her she needed to do skin grafting to create fat around her breast implants. She asked if she could take it from her arms and the doctor told her, "No. I am not able to do any liposuction on an area that has lymphedema; it is not medically approved or safe."

Because she had done the full body years earlier, she didn't have enough fat to make the breasts, and she had to have several surgeries before her breasts were finished. Her anger was larger than life and affecting every area of her life.

In 2010, she had taken The Quinn Essentials Workshop in Los Angeles. She really wanted to improve the quality of her life and learn to manage her anger. When we got to the last tool, she had an emotional reaction. She realized how much letting go she needed to do and became committed to working on herself with these 9 tools. Focusing on what she could control and being grateful for being alive was a great place to start. She worked every day on letting go of anger and disempowering thought, which led to the place of letting go completely.

Nine years later, after taking a long break from surgeries and doctors, she had to remove the implants and needed fat to recreate her breasts. She scheduled the surgery in 2019. At the consultation, the doctor mentioned there would need to be another skin grafting. The doctor suggested they take it from her arms! She said, "Doctor, you told me 15 years ago I couldn't take it from my arms because I had lymphedema." Then the doctor said, "That changed a few years ago. Not only do we have the technology to do liposuction with lymphedema, but it is also now *an approved and safe treatment of lymphedema." Needless to say, she had a successful surgery with the grafting from her arms.*

This woman has taken this workshop at least five times since 2010 and understands the power of letting go. She believes releasing her anger allowed her to create the space and magical experience of her 2019 "Happily Ever After" ending. She is happy to be alive, grateful for the advances in science and technology and is a believer in the power of letting go.

Letting go changes your story.

I know women who go back to their high school reunion and are consumed with negative thoughts about people they haven't seen in 25 years. They say things like, "I just hate her. She didn't like me on the volleyball team." It was 25 years ago! Okay, she was mean – 25 years ago. Let go of all that. I worked with an actor who told me that when they first came to town, they had auditions with a casting director and now, 10 years later, they don't want to go in and see them because they are sure they hated them the first time around. They were willing to not follow through with an opportunity that could change their career because of something that happened 10 years ago. Do you see how we do this? It's exhausting! Holding on to things can impact us and prevent us from the wonderful things the Universe has for us in our future.

Instead, we hold onto our stories – especially when that story has defined us for so long. But I want to ask you, how is being attached to that story working out for you? (It is probably your life's biggest obstacle.)

I had asked the woman going to the class reunion to let go of the past and try to stay present knowing that 25 years has passed and perhaps the person had grown up. Not only did she enjoy herself but the woman from the volleyball team also apologized for being mean in high school. She would never have been able to receive the apology or have a good time if she hadn't let go.

Your story does not define you. What defines you is what you decide. Tony Robbins has a wonderful saying, *"The only meaning anything has is the meaning you give it."* What meaning are you giving to your stories? Our stories are moments in time that we have already lived and by letting them go, we create the space necessary to accomplish our dreams.

In teaching workshops to women from all walks of life, the biggest obstacle to not having their dreams come true is what they are refusing to release. When we let go, we experience a freedom, an exhalation that aligns us with our divine birthright to Receive. When we as women receive, we create and that is truly our gift to this world.

Let Go! Receive! Create! repeat...

Tools in Motion

1. Look at your accomplishment list and ask yourself is there anything you must let go of to receive your dream? Use the questions in this chapter as guidelines to ask yourself powerful questions regarding letting go. Take note and begin work on the first step.

2. Let go of one small thing a day. A thought? A judgment? A mistake? Keep a journal of what you notice and experience.

3. Look back on your life and remind yourself of every good thing that happened to you by letting go.

4. Make a "To Let Go" List – and write down things you are holding on to and work to release them one at a time.

Good to Know

1. To let go is to have faith.

2. Letting go doesn't mean giving up.

3. I am open to everything and attached to nothing.

4. Letting go is power.

5. Your amount of personal freedom is expanded by how much you will Let Go.

6. Letting go changes your story.

Continuing the Conversation

For more information on this tool, please join me for a video, which will open you up further to the practice of letting go.

http://www.thequinnessentials.com/letgo/

or scan QR code

Epilogue
Life with your Toolkit

Since I've started living and sharing The Quinn Essentials, I have been a witness to what can happen when women are empowered and have the tools to guide them. I am certain these tools will guide you to a deeper relationship with yourself, the creation of loving and safe communities and an empowered life of success and happiness. The 9 tools are a practice. You can practice them every day along with me and you have the rest of your life to perfect them.

You are probably thinking, "A practice? Every Day?" "I barely have time to eat!" Even more of a reason to live your life with this Toolkit. Don't you think I already know you are exhausted? I know you have a lot on your plate right now. (Take a breath.) Your life is probably filled with challenge after challenge, but I believe with all my heart that you have the power as a receiver to create magic. (Exhale.)

These tools have created communities of women who help each other and speak the same empowerment language. You are now a part of this group and are welcomed with open arms. There are several ways to access and receive support through platforms, workshops and working with a certified Quinn Essentials coach.

As this book ends and your life with your Toolkit begins, I want to leave you with a few suggestions to help you work with your Toolkit.

1. Make a list of the tools in order as a type of check list. Put them up somewhere where you can see them each day. Seeing them in this order, they will begin to become your roadmap of support and accomplishment. Just being aware of the tools begins to shift something with in your being. (Women have even made canvases for their offices that include their I AMs as well as the tools themselves.)

2. Go back into your Toolkit and notice the tool that felt the hardest for you. Give that tool extra attention every day for 30 days. Yes, 30 days! When I first began to share these tools, we did them in a class that lasted 9 months. Each woman who took the class was given a new tool every month and she had 30 days to focus on them. As you know, I believe that what we focus on expands and when focusing on a tool for 30 days, you can have amazing results and it will become easier. (I promise!)

   Use the language you learned in the book at least once a day. For example, "I would like to receive your assistance with _____." "I will require _____ to move forward with this situation." "Would you see to this for me?"

   This empowered language will keep the tools fresh in your mind and will yield amazing results.

I authentically use these tools in every moment of my life. Life is hard for every woman! Over the past two years, mine has been filled with life-shattering curve balls (as yours, I'm sure). From finding my beloved dog dead on the floor, to global pandemics and lockdowns, to my closest friend diagnosed with stage 4 cancer and to my younger brother suddenly passing away.

All I could do was start from the beginning, take a deep breath and ask, "What one thing can I receive right now that will create peace and support for me in this situation?" "Where can I receive support from when I can't even get up off the floor?" But, like a miracle from above, I was able to stand on a foundation of my I AMs, Listen, focus on my Self-Acceptance to stay strong, Connect, Ask for help, Visualize peaceful solutions with prayer, speak gratefully with Empowered Words and Let Go of what I could not control. This Toolkit saved me!

In this book, I made a lot of promises with this work and I take that very seriously. Make promises to yourself today, feel free to share them with me as I hope you will keep in touch and be an active participant in my "Accomplishment Group" community (AG for short). I know it takes work to take our power back, remember who we really are and interrupt disempowering beliefs and behaviors; but when we do, our life becomes filled with happiness, peace and love.

Here are few more promises I make to you today:
1. I will always be an open book. #beingopen

2. I will always share my growth and challenges and not ever make you think "I've got it all together."
#workingthroughmymess #notperfect #alwaysseeking
3. I will always keep using my Toolkit. #thequinnessentials
4. I will always keep believing in you. #youcandoit #youareenough
5. I will never judge you because I know if you could do anything better, you would do it. #startover #keepgrowing #getbackup #askforhelp
6. I will always think in terms of the collective "WE."
#womenempoweringwomen
#community
#wearestrongertogether
#findyourpeople

Again, I am overwhelmed with gratitude that you read this book and allowed me to share The Quinn Essentials with you. Your life matters to me. Your dreams matter to me. You are a part of a sacred empowerment movement of women who are going to save and heal this world, we need you!

I wish for you an empowered life with your Toolkit. May you let go a little every day to open space, receive all your accomplishments and create magic for yourself and the world. (Thank you again, Dalai Lama.)

With respect and love, Andrea

Notes

"A Return to Love" – Marianne Williamson (Chapter 4)

"Creative Visualization" – Shakti Gawain (Chapter 6)

"She Let Go" – Reverend Safire Rose (Chapter 9)

Terms and Definitions

Lady Shame – the shame women feel by the social and cultural standards put on them whereby we experience negative evaluation of self. Created by Rita Merson 2017.

Good Girl Syndrome – Characteristics of good girl syndrome is fear of disappointing others, fear of speaking out for fear of hurting others, must always excel, avoid conflict, obey rules and find it difficult to refuse. It also includes not wanting to bother anyone and playing it small and safe.

Ask-itis – The self-imposed sick feeling we have that creates so many negative thoughts and emotions when it comes to asking for what we want to receive. Created by Andrea Quinn 2016

When Syndrome – Combination of symptoms that delays taking action in the present moment to the future by projecting tasks onto ourselves that must be achieved before we can receive. Created by Andrea Quinn 2017

Endgame – It is a term developed for chess, a final stage for a game. In life, it is synonymous with your legacy.

Snippet Visualization – A short visualization created as a moment in time to experience by sharing with others for support. Created by Andrea Quinn 2008

Snippet Party – A group of people in a party-like atmosphere that share Snippets to support each other.

Acknowledgements

Thinking of all the acknowledgments I want to give, I am finding it overwhelming. I have so many people to thank that I have tears in my eyes right now and a warm feeling in my heart just beginning this process. The questions are coming up for me like "What if I miss someone?" "What if I hurt someone by not including them?" "Why does 'Thank You' seem so small when gratitude is so huge?" Taking an in-breath, I am pushing past these questions from my mind and dropping down into my heart where I am taking an exhale, letting go and opening this chapter.

There have been so many people who have contributed to the expansion of my life and these tools that if I thanked everyone I want to acknowledge, this chapter would be larger than the entire book!

Let me start by saying "Thank You" to the thousands of women since 2008 who have trusted me to share these tools, utilize the Toolkit and implement receiving into their lives. You have shared this work with countless friends, family members and co-workers. My heart is expanding thinking of all of you.

I want to give a special thanks to all the ladies who assisted me during the groups and worked to help me each month set up and manage the rooms, I couldn't have done it without you. I want to especially thank Kristine Louise DelGado, Nora Ellingwood,

Angela Espinosa-Johnson, Lisa Kenney, Debra Rogers, Amanda Shi-Werts, Ani Williams and Kasandra Carlson-Zimbron, for being my first group in 2008 who sparked it all! To Evelyn Jackson, your courage and poetry gave the first spark a flame, there are no words.

Elysia Skye, you are an Angel Fairy in my life who has brought love and magic to my work. Dr. Hillary Smith, your guidance and love has taught me to care about myself and health in a way that holds space for the sacred feminine, I am eternally grateful. Chandra Scofield, my healing fairy who saw all the good coming as you covered me with needles, brought in sound and light to heal me and befriended me and my tools unconditionally.

To the men in my life who have believed in my curriculum and have not only promoted my tools but paid for women to take the workshops. So much gratitude to Juvan, Gavin, Doug, Drew, Jeff, Joe, Aaron, David, Paul, Yawar, Jim, Nick and countless others. It is so empowering to know that there are so many men who support women and their empowerment!

A special note of spiritual gratitude to Elizabeth Morales, Sylvie Vaught and Gabrielle Yuro who have had my back since we met and have encouraged me to keep reaching for the stars.
Cindy Garcia Rogel and Zakiya Matthews, you both stood by me, took care of me and managed all my groups and final nights for many years. I was able to teach in such a powerful way because you were supporting me. I love you both.

Debbie Geltner and Joel Sansone, you rock! Thank you for your vision, support and patience. You both are always there for me at a moment's notice and I wouldn't have a digital presence without you.

This book wouldn't have happened if it wasn't for the next wonderful ladies.

First, Cindy Yantis, I could write an entire page about you! You were my first coaching client and told everyone about me to start my business. You have encouraged me to write this book in ways that only a Fairy Godmother could. For years, you worked on me to create this book and I value all you have added with your Creative Jam sessions and daily guidance. So many lives, so much gratitude, so much love.

Secondly, Sara Glasser, what can I say? You are a fantastic writer who helped me on this journey with all your heart and soul. You took care of my tools as if they were your own and made me family. You are a magical lady and I can't begin to thank you properly with mere words. Thank you for holding such space for me – FGC forever!

Next, Michaela Kennedy, we have been connected since we met. I never dreamed that I would be lucky enough to have you support me the way you do. Thank you for everything you did with this project and everything you do for my business and my life. This planet is lucky you were born and thank you for all projects you do worldwide to make this world a better place.

And finally, Linda Sivertsen, the Book Mama, you loved this book before it was written. Thank you for the confidence in my writing since your Carmel Writing Retreat I attended. You were always a champion of my work and in my corner.

Another group of firsts I would like to thank is my first team of certified Quinn Essentials Coaches. As the community expands, the women who are lucky enough to work with you will be transformed because of your intelligence, light and hearts: Sara Glasser, Cari Rose, Susie Goliti, Lisa Gould, Maria Mahboubi, Shelia Melody, Haleh Shoa, Elysia Skye, Meryl Russo and Cindy Yantis. You are all amazing coaches in your own practices and I am beyond grateful you wanted to coach these tools.

To my forever crew, Heather Kelly, Belinda Wise, Lisa Kenney, Karen Sobul Miller, Stephanie Young and Michelle Pietroforte, I have grown up with all of you through many decades, many adventures and many lives. I love you more than words.

Zonnie Thierbach, you are my guardian Angel and I love you more than Paris!

Ilias Fiakka, thank you for always taking care of me, even while I am annoying you.

Erika, Melissa, Jasmin, Mckenzie, Genna, Violet and Ashley; watching all of you grow up has been such a gift to my life. I have learned so much from each of you and am so proud of the powerful women you are becoming for this world.

Valerie Williamson, since the moment we met in Junior high your energy and light has been contagious. Your support and love has guided me through each decade of my life. You are a part of my family, every group, friendship circle, and community I have. Everyone who knows me, knows you. Your strength inspires me daily and your confidence in me has never wavered. I love you more!

To my sister in this lifetime, Nora Ellingwood. From the first class to today, you have been by my side supporting my growth and these tools. You have been there for all the groups and have helped me put on too many events to count. You have attended everything I have ever done and your love and belief in me at times have filled rooms. We have an amazing family together with our husbands, kids and extended members; for that I thank God every day. What you do for my nieces, mom, cousins, aunt and uncles and everyone in my life is otherworldly. Love you so much my sister. I am Grateful.

To Brent Ellingwood, thank you for all the times you showed up to be of service to the community of women. You are a Knight!

To my aunts Annie Ayala and Carmen Morley, you have supported me my entire life. Thank you both for traveling all those years to come to my women's events and supporting me and my community wholeheartedly. You are both Angels in my life. And to my cousin Jennifer Gonzales, you carry on the love from our family with such wisdom and grace.

To my soul mate and husband Chris Wilson, thank you for all the love and support over the years. You have always helped me to be better and grow in ways that I couldn't have imagined. I feel respected and honored by you every day. You have the patience of Job! Many events for these tools were hosted by you to support not only me but all the women who were in the workshops. To have a husband who respects and admires women is a dream come true. You are a Warrior of Light! I am beyond grateful for the life we create together. Thank you, my beloved!

To my dad, Merle, thank you for the guidance and your love of knowledge. I still hear and feel you every day and know what an important part of this whole process you have been.

My mom, Antoinette "Lovie" Runolfson, you have been the shining star to light the way for me to grow as a woman. You taught me love, courage, strength, forgiveness and every goodness a woman can have. Everything I do, I do for you because everything you ever did was for me. Thank you for the unconditional love I couldn't give myself. The family of women I received because of you is so sacred to me that I work to honor the legacy every day. You gave me my first women's group with your sisters and because of that, I will continue to create sisterhood the rest of my life. Love you. Love you. Love you. You are the "Wind Beneath my Wings."

About the Author

Andrea Quinn is a Certified Life and Business Coach, Empowerment Specialist, Motivational Speaker and Author with over 15 years of experience. She holds a mirror for some of the world's most innovative individuals and corporations who consider her to be one of their most trusted advisors. Her datebook reads like a Who's Who in Entertainment, Publishing, Music, Silicon Valley, Wall Street and the Healing Arts.

Since 2008, she has shared her original curriculum "The Quinn Essentials" with thousands of women all over the globe in live and digital workshops. Her commitment to female empowerment is her greatest passion and has built a community for women where they receive support, inclusion and relationships, which assist them in creating and sustaining their best lives.

Andrea lives in Los Angeles, California with her husband, Chris and their many fur children.

Andreaquinncoaching.com

Instagram – andreaquinncoaching

Twitter @AQCoaching

Facebook.com/andreaquinncoaching

Resources

For more information on upcoming digital or live workshops, go to https://thequinnessentials.com

To continue receiving support with the tools to accomplish your dreams, work with a certified Quinn Essentials Coach – for more information email: coaching@thequinnessentials.com

If you are interested in corporate programs, motivational speaking or business coaching, email: info@andreaquinncoaching.com

Made in USA - Kendallville, IN
60551_9781734734201
04.18.2022 1249